'I don't have much experience with dogs,' I told

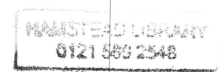

Melissa Wareham always loved dogs and wanted to work with them. Her life changed for ever on the day she got her first job at Battersea Dogs & Cats Home. To clean out the kennels!

Meet some of the wonderful doggy friends Melissa met over the years in this heart-warming real-life tale.

Take Me Home

Tales of Battersea dogs

Melissa Wareham

RED FOX BOOKS

TAKE ME HOME
A RED FOX BOOK 978 1 849 41392 3

First published in Great Britain by Red Fox,
an imprint of Random House Children's Books
A Random House Group Company

This edition published 2011

1 3 5 7 9 10 8 6 4 2

Set in 14/20pt Bembo by Falcon Oast Graphic Art Ltd.

Red Fox Books are published by Random House Children's Books,
61–63 Uxbridge Road, London W5 5SA

www.**kids**at**randomhouse**.co.uk
www.**rbooks**.co.uk

Addresses for companies within The Random House Group Limited can be
found at: www.randomhouse.co.uk/offices.htm

THE RANDOM HOUSE GROUP Limited Reg. No. 954009

A CIP catalogue record for this book is available from the British Library.

Printed in the UK by CPI Bookmarque, Croydon, CR0 4TD

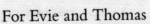
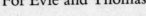

For Evie and Thomas

CHAPTER ONE

Like a Dog with a Bone

'No! Absolutely not! There is no way we are getting a dog!' my mum said, turning redder and redder. She was beginning to look like a tomato.

'It's not fair,' I wailed. 'All my friends have got one.'

'And all your friends have lost interest in them and now their mums and dads have to walk them, feed them and clear up after them.' Mum was so horrified by the idea of getting a dog that her eyes were nearly popping out of her head.

'Your mother's right,' my dad added from behind his newspaper. 'You'd only get bored with a dog.'

But she wasn't right and neither was he, and if only they could see into my heart, they'd realize it was aching for a dog and that I would *never, ever* lose interest in it or get bored with it.

I was eight years old and ever since I could remember, having a dog was all I could think about. Whenever I was due a free wish – from eating strawberries for the first time every summer, to seeing a black cat or catching snowflakes – it was always the same: 'I wish that I had a dog.' I never imagined there might be a day when I'd have 700!

We never had any animals when I was growing up; my family just didn't get any. I tried to persuade my older brother that getting a dog would be an excellent idea; double pester-power would surely make my parents cave in.

'Go on,' I said to him. 'It'll be brilliant. We can share the dog – you could have it Monday to Wednesday and I'll have it for the rest of the time.'

'What do I want with a dog?' he said. 'I'd rather have a new computer, thank you very much.'

I couldn't understand this. Why would anyone want a new computer over a dog? You can't take a computer for a walk; it won't play *fetch* with you and it certainly wouldn't make a very good best friend either. In my eyes nothing could compare with having a real, live dog.

Everything I owned was doggy: dog slippers, dog lunch box, dog pyjamas, dog books and dog duvet and pillows. I had everything but *the dog*!

I knew everything there was to know about them too, like:

- they all have pink tongues except for chow-chows who have bluish-black tongues.
- basenjis are the only dogs that can't bark.
- and Newfoundland dogs actually have webbed feet!

Even though my parents were impressed by all my dog knowledge, I knew they'd never give in. But then again, neither would I. I was like a dog with a bone.

'*Pleeease*,' I begged, my voice rising to a frustrated screech, 'I won't get bored, I promise. I've saved up all my pocket money for the last two years and *I'll* buy the dog. I can even pay for its collar and lead, some toys and its food and water bowls,' I squeaked, barely able to speak.

'No,' came their terrible and very final-sounding reply. 'It's not about paying for stuff. It's about us having to look after the dog once the novelty has worn off. Dogs are a big responsibility, you know.'

I knew that! I'd been dreaming about having this responsibility for ever. They just didn't understand and I was afraid they never would.

I've always loved dogs. From the tips of their cold, wet noses and their big fluffy ears, right down to their four furry feet and wagging tails.

In fact, my first ever memory involved a dog.

When I was three years old my mum and I went shopping. Outside the shop was an enormous German shepherd dog, like the ones the police have. My mum was inside, busy filling up her shopping basket with horrid green vegetables I knew she was buying for me to eat later, so I wandered out to the front of the shop to say hello to the dog. He was as big as me, his fur was black and brown and he had enormous paws. Our brown eyes met at exactly the same height, but with his long, pointy ears he was taller than me. I didn't feel scared at all; in fact, I took a step closer to him. He looked right into my eyes whilst sniffing the air in my direction. I took another step closer until we were nose-to-nose.

'*Woof!*' I said, trying to speak to him in his own language. Somewhere inside the shop I heard a shopping basket clatter to the ground. Four potatoes and a cabbage came rolling out towards me. The German shepherd dog yawned a gigantic yawn, almost big enough to swallow me whole. His breath smelled terrible, like dog food, and he had the biggest teeth I'd ever seen. *My, what big teeth you have, Grandma*, I thought to myself. They were so long and white and sharp that any wolf would have been proud to own them. After this very impressive yawn, he just turned away, rather bored. I left him and toddled back into the shop where I found my mum frozen to the spot, her hands covering her open mouth, a terrified look on her face.

★

A week before I turned nine, my parents asked me what I wanted for my birthday.

'A dog,' I said, as if they didn't know.

'Anything else?' they enquired hopefully.

'No.'

The morning of my birthday arrived and I padded down the stairs, still in my pyjamas, still sleepy, hair sticking out in every direction. My parents were waiting for me in the kitchen. They were acting very strangely, standing side by side and grinning, as though they were hiding something behind them. I knew that look on my dad's face. It was his 'you are going to *love* this' face.

A thought too wonderful to even hope for raced across my mind. Had they finally given in and got me a dog? No, surely they couldn't have – could they? They were so excited I began to think that maybe they had.

'Close your eyes and hold out your hands,' my mum said, barely able to control her voice. My heart was pounding as visions flooded through my head. Would it be a boy or a girl puppy? What colour would it be? How old? How big? Would its ears be pointed or floppy? I held out my shaking hands, hardly daring to breathe.

'Hold them flat and still, you don't want to drop him,' said my dad.

Him? Oh my goodness, they *had* . . . I held my hands out as flat and as still as I possibly could. I could almost feel my new puppy's warm furry bottom in my hands.

Something was very gently placed in my upturned palms.

Hmm. This is strange, I thought to myself, eyes still closed. I could feel a cool, smooth, hard, flat object. It weighed about the same as my school lunch box (before I'd eaten the contents). For a terrible moment, I thought it *was* my lunch box, or a new one at any rate.

Then I slowly opened one eye. I didn't really know what I was seeing so I opened both eyes. I looked down upon something resembling a soldier's helmet. It was greeny-brown with rather pretty circular patterns on it. Right at that moment, a head, followed by a tail and four scaly legs with sharp claws at the ends, shot out from beneath the helmet. I was so shocked I screamed and almost dropped it. The head, four legs and tail flew back in – and then it dawned on me.

My parents had got me a tortoise!

I felt like screaming and crying and slamming doors, because in my heart of hearts I knew what this meant – this was as good as it was going to get; they were never, *ever* going to let me have a dog – or anything with fur, for that matter.

We named the tortoise Spiro and I tried to love him, but apart from the fact he had four legs, a head and a tail, nothing about him resembled a dog.

I tried to walk him but he was too slow.

When I called him he just wouldn't come. I threw a ball for him, which he wouldn't bring back.

And when I tried to tell him my problems, he got bored and retreated back into his mobile home.

At school the following week, a lady from Guide Dogs for the Blind came to our assembly. She brought a Labrador called Dillon with her; he had beautiful brown eyes, honey-coloured fur and a long pink tongue. She explained how, with special training, dogs like Dillon could help their blind owners do lots of things they couldn't do without a guide dog.

'Dillon is only one year old and still in training,' said the lady, 'but he's learning to help people cross the road, get on and off buses and even help them with their supermarket shopping.' Dillon showed us how by picking up a can of baked beans with his teeth and putting it into a shopping basket!

When we were allowed to ask questions, I was the first to put up my hand.

'Where did you get Dillon from?' I asked his handler.

'I found him when he was just eight weeks old at a place called Battersea Dogs & Cats Home. It's a rescue centre in southwest London where hundreds of lost and unwanted dogs are taken,' she explained. 'The poor little fellow had been wandering down a busy London street all on his own. He might have been run over had a kind lady not picked him up and taken him to Battersea Dogs Home.'

Dillon was one of the lucky ones – he was chosen to become a guide dog – but I wondered about all the other dogs at Battersea that still needed looking after, needed to find new homes.

It was a mystery to me how so many could all fit under one roof. And in London too! It would be much easier in the country; there would be lots of fields for them to run around in, but where could that many dogs run in London? I thought about offering our back garden, but I didn't think my dad would be very happy to let all those dogs run loose in his vegetable patch!

At the end of the talk we got to stroke Dillon. He loved all the attention, wagging his tail throughout.

Our homework was to write about Guide Dogs for the Blind and the work they did. My teacher gave me an A*! It was the only A* I ever got.

A year later, when I was ten, my dad asked me what I wanted to be when I grew up. That was easy.

'A vet,' I said. 'I want to work with dogs and especially help the sick ones.'

'Ew!' said my brother. 'Why would you want to work with animals? They smell, they poo, they puke and they've got fleas.'

'They sound a bit like you!' I replied, which earned me a clip round the ear from my dad.

Becoming a vet was easier said than done. I tried to work hard at school and pass my exams, but most of the time I found myself staring out of the window, daydreaming about dogs, wishing I had one and trying to work out how on earth I could get one.

All my friends at school wanted to be footballers or pop stars, but I didn't see the point of that. Why kick a ball around if it wasn't for a dog to chase? And if you wanted to sing, you could just do it in the shower.

My school days flew by and before I knew it, it was time to leave. I passed some exams, but not enough to become a vet. This little hiccup didn't put me off my dream of working with dogs, though. If I couldn't be a vet, I'd help them in some other way.

I reached for the phone. I knew exactly who to call.

CHAPTER TWO

Hundreds and Hundreds
of Hounds

Since finding out about Battersea Dogs Home,
I'd always wanted to visit, but you had to go
with an adult and no one would ever take me.
They were all hoping I'd forget about having a
dog, but I wouldn't.

I couldn't. Could you?

I knew I'd have to wait until I was a grown-
up before I'd be able to go on my own, so I
waited. I waited and waited and waited until

finally my time came . . .

It was a freezing-cold February morning and even my coat, hat and gloves couldn't keep out the winter chill. I didn't care though. I was sitting on the top deck of the number 36 bus on my way to Battersea Dogs Home, and not just for a look around – I was going for a job interview! I had just left school and couldn't think of anywhere in the world I'd rather work.

I walked into the reception area and was immediately greeted by the smell of dogs. I took a long, slow breath and let it out through a contented smile – this place felt more like home to me than my own home.

'Can I help you?' asked the lady behind the counter. I was just about to answer when a large, shaggy dog, also behind the counter, jumped up and wagged its tail at me.

'Hello!' I said to the dog.

'Her name's Katie,' said the lady. 'She's very friendly if you want to stroke her.'

I took off one glove, stood on tiptoes and reached over the counter. Katie snuffled my hand and wagged her tail even harder. I tried to stroke her ear, but I couldn't find it under all that hair!

'What type of dog is she?' I asked.

'She's a mongrel; a mixture of lots of breeds,' said the lady. 'Her mother was a collie mixed with a terrier and her father was a German shepherd mixed with a spaniel.'

'Wow, that's quite a mixture!' I said, impressed.

'Are you here to give a dog a home?' asked the lady.

'No, not yet. I'd love to, but I don't think my mum would be too pleased if I came home with a dog! I've come to see Mr Wadman Taylor about a job.'

'Well, you obviously like dogs,' she said, 'and that's a pretty good place to start if you want to work here!' She made a quick phone call and within thirty seconds a tall man with white hair and a matching beard appeared at the door. He was dressed in a green three-piece suit and he puffed away earnestly on a pipe.

Mr Wadman Taylor was in charge of Battersea Dogs Home and he was also the head vet. *He must have studied hard at school*, I thought to myself. He showed me up to his office and pointed to the chair he wanted me to sit in.

In between me and the chair was a dog bed containing two terriers. They must have thought I wanted to get in their bed because when they saw me, they stood up and began growling, guarding their basket.

Mr Wadman Taylor assured me they were harmless (with him, maybe), but as I took a step towards my chair, they both leaped out of the bed and began attacking my feet! I hadn't had any proper experience with dogs before and I wasn't exactly sure what to do, but I decided that I wasn't going to let these two overstuffed snarling cushions spoil my chances of getting my dream job.

I shut my eyes and hoped for the best, inching my way over to the chair. I had ten toes, after all; surely it wouldn't matter too much if I lost one or two. Holding my breath, I managed to make it over to the chair where, by mistake, I sat on the oldest of Mr Wadman Taylor's terriers. He was blind and deaf and as I made contact with him, he made a sort of farting bagpipe sound, but luckily no harm was done. We got on with the interview.

The room was quite dark, with green leather chairs; there were dog beds everywhere. The desk was piled high with books and paperwork. There were photographs on the walls of handsome hounds, proudly posing with large silver trophies. I couldn't decide if the room smelled more of dog or pipe tobacco, but something about it made me feel very safe and happy.

'What do you know about Battersea Dogs Home?' Mr Wadman Taylor asked me.

'Well,' I began, 'I know you have about seven

hundred dogs here. Most of them are stray dogs that have been found wandering the streets, but some have been brought straight into Battersea by owners who didn't want them or couldn't look after them any more.'

'That's right,' he replied. 'Stray dogs are sometimes brought here by members of the public who have found them.' I thought back to Dillon, the guide dog, and remembered that was how he came to be at Battersea. 'Other times, dog wardens bring them in. They are paid by the council to keep dogs from running around the streets and causing accidents. Sometimes the dogs are genuinely lost and their owners come to claim them, but sadly a lot are just thrown out and left to fend for themselves,' he added.

This seemed very unfair to me. All I'd ever wanted was a dog and to find out that some people, who were lucky enough to have them, could just throw them away like this was almost too much to bear. Dogs rely on us to look after them, to feed them and protect them. Now I was more determined than ever to help.

'What do you do with all these hundreds of dogs?' I asked, bewildered. 'What happens to the ones that aren't claimed?'

'Well,' he said, 'there are four main things that Battersea Dogs Home tries to do. They all begin with the letter R so we call them *The four Rs*. Any idea what they might be?' he asked me.

I'd survived Mr Wadman Taylor's terriers; perhaps this was my next test. I thought for a while and took a deep breath.

'Erm, let's see. The first thing Battersea does is *rescue* dogs.'

'Correct,' he said. 'That's the first R.'

'Then' – I swallowed hard – 'Battersea tries to *reunite* them with their owners.'

'Yes! Reuniting is just another word for when they are claimed by their owners,' he said. 'That's the second R. Two out of two – not bad! What about the third R?'

I thought hard. 'If you cannot reunite the

dog with its owner, does Battersea try to *rehome* it with a new owner?'

'You're right, another *R*!' he said. 'Thankfully lots of kind-hearted people come to Battersea every day to give one of our dogs a loving new home where we hope it'll be happy for the rest of its life. But there's still one more *R*,' he said, testing me again.

I was stumped. I just couldn't think what the other R might be.

'It's what we call *rehabilitation*,' he said.

'What exactly is that?' I asked.

'Well,' he said, having another puff of his pipe, 'some dogs that come into Battersea are very nervous and have to be taught that it's OK to trust people. Others can sometimes be aggressive and we have to train them out of this unwanted behaviour before we rehome them. Both of these are examples of rehabilitation,' he said.

That made sense. I desperately wanted to be a part of this wonderful organization.

'I don't have much experience with dogs,' I told Mr Wadman Taylor, 'as my parents wouldn't let me have one, but I'm a fast learner, really keen and I have loved dogs since the day I was born.'

He seemed convinced and offered me a job as a kennel maid, where I would be responsible for cleaning out, feeding and walking about fifty dogs. Wow, *fifty dogs*! I couldn't believe it!

Mr Wadman Taylor asked me if I wanted to have a tour of Battersea Dogs Home and see the dogs. Of course I did!

I was very excited, and as we walked towards the large kennel block, I heard the dogs barking. I couldn't wait to get in there.

The kennel block was large and bright and smelled of disinfectant, dog food and dog, all rolled into one. It was about as wide as the side of a bus and twice as long, with a concrete aisle running down the middle. Fifty kennels with metal bars at the front lined either side of the aisle. Most of them contained two or three dogs of all shapes and sizes; loud, spotty dogs, small, shaggy ones, lean, hungry dogs and scared, whimpering hounds all in together.

In some kennels there were four or five puppies jumping all over each other, messing about and having a whale of a time. In others, there were fat oldies who were fast asleep.

There were hundreds of dogs everywhere and I should have been delighted, I was, after all, surrounded by the creatures I loved. But to see them in cages and know they'd all been abandoned was really heartbreaking, and I couldn't understand how these beautiful, intelligent, faithful creatures could have ended up this way.

'When do I start, Mr Wadman Taylor?' I said, eager to begin helping.

'How about tomorrow morning?' he asked, through a fluffy white-bearded grin. 'Say eight o'clock?'

'Done!' I said. 'See you tomorrow.' I felt like the cat who'd got the cream.

'Oh,' I said as an afterthought, 'do you have cats here too?'

'Yes,' replied Mr Wadman Taylor. 'About a hundred!'

As I sat on the bus home, I couldn't stop smiling, even though my teeth were chattering with the cold. I'd gone from always wanting a dog but never being allowed to have one, to having hundreds of my very own! I couldn't believe it – just wait till I told my mum!

CHAPTER THREE

Tulip Rides the Bus

'How many?' said my mum, with eyes as wide as saucers. 'You must be stark, raving mad!'

Even so, at eight o'clock the next morning I was standing inside the gates of Battersea Dogs Home where a large German shepherd was charging towards me, barking his head off. I looked around, but there was nobody to rescue me. When he was about an arm's length away from me he stopped barking. *Phew*, I thought, until he replaced his noisy bark with a terrifying growl.

'GGGGRRRRRRRRRRRRRRRRRR!'

If that wasn't scary enough, he also showed me his rather large, fierce-looking fangs. So far my first day at Battersea Dogs Home wasn't quite going to plan!

'Hello, boy,' I said, hoping to appeal to his good side. 'What's your name then?' He stood firm, still grumbling away.

'Jimmy! Jimmy, come here,' called a tall lady with long hair, running down the yard after him. 'Sorry,' she said. 'He doesn't like strangers.' And with that she put him on a lead and he was gone.

Phew, that was close! Now that the coast was clear I took a step forward, but didn't see the huge pile of steaming dog poo in front of me and trod right in it. *Oh dear*, I thought to myself, *I suppose things can only get better.*

'Hullo!' shouted Mr Wadman Taylor, who was waving to me from halfway down the yard.

I stamped my foot, trying to get the poo off my shoe as best I could and limped over to him. He was standing next to a lady dressed in a blue sweatshirt, blue jeans and green Wellington boots. The sweatshirt had a small picture of a dog on the front with the words *Battersea Dogs Home* written underneath.

'This is Jacky,' he said. 'She'll show you what to do.'

Jacky was a little smaller than me and had short dark hair with a blonde flash running through it. She gave me a big smile and took me over to the block where she and I would be working. Before we went in she handed me my new uniform, which was identical to hers. I changed in the staff room and stood facing the mirror. I looked like a proper kennel maid. Jacky came in and said, 'Hmm, not bad, but there's something missing.' Then she handed me my very own dog lead and kennel key on a chain. If I'd had a tail, right then it would have been wagging like mad!

'You'll also need some of these,' she said, handing me a packet of dog treats. They were called Schmackos and the label read *Roast Beef-Flavoured*. They smelled just like my mum's Sunday roast.

'Have you ever worked in kennels before?' she asked.

'No,' I replied. I didn't like to admit I'd never even had a dog before.

'OK.' She went on to tell me the duties of a kennel maid, which were:

- cleaning out – there are too many dogs to take for a walk so sometimes they go to the toilet in their kennel.
- feeding – they get two meals a day; the skinny ones get three.
- exercising – we walk as many as we can in the time we've got.
- grooming – if any of them need a bath, that's our job too.
- socializing – some of the dogs are very

frightened and it's up to us to show them life isn't so bad!

'Think you can handle it?' she said.

'Oh yes,' I replied, barely able to contain my excitement. Being a kennel maid was everything I'd ever dreamed of and a whole lot more besides! I was going to love it here at Battersea Dogs Home.

Jacky and I marched over to our kennel block and stood outside the door.

'Ready?' she asked me.

'Ready.' I nodded.

When Jacky opened the heavy metal door, I was nearly deafened by the noise. A hundred hungry hounds all wanting their breakfast sounded more like a thousand. To make matters worse, the kennel block was right underneath a railway so trains were constantly clattering backwards and forward overhead. But what was much worse than the noise was the smell! The dogs had last been cleaned out at five o'clock the night before, which was when the kennel maids went home. That meant they'd had fifteen hours of pooing time, and it was everywhere! All over the kennel floor, all over the kennel bars and all over their paws, so if I went in there and they jumped up at me, it would be all over me too!

But when I saw my first dog, the noise of the barking and the trains and the smell of dog poo immediately disappeared. He was a little black-and-white mongrel, about six months old.

'What's his name?' I shouted to Jacky.

'He doesn't have one,' she yelled back. 'He only came in yesterday and he's a stray. You can name him if you want.'

I kneeled down to his level and he pushed himself against the bars. He was mainly white, but he had two black splodges, one around each eye, two black ears and a black tail. His ears and paws were way too big for him. He had soft, fuzzy puppy fur and big brown eyes that were begging me to touch him.

I raised my hand through the bars to stroke him, but he ducked as though he was expecting to be hit. Jacky explained that I should always start by stroking a dog on its chest rather than its head and that I shouldn't look it straight in the eye, as this is less worrying for them.

Through the bars I gently stroked his chest, working my way up to a scratch behind one of those big ears. He loved it. I remembered the dog treats that Jacky had given me and reached into my pocket. I pulled out a Schmacko. It smelled delicious and I was tempted to have a nibble! Instead, I pushed it through the bars. The puppy took it ever so gently, but once he had it, he gobbled it up. I don't think it touched the sides!

'I'm going to call you Sunny,' I said, and he licked his chops and wagged his bum at me.

Jacky handed me a bucket, some disinfectant and a broom, showed me where the tap was to fill up my bucket and wished me luck.

'Looks like Sunny's got an upset stomach,'

she said. 'Make sure you clean it all up.'

The long kennel block had an aisle running through it and Jacky decided that we'd take a side each, which meant I'd be cleaning fifty kennels. I had better get a move on if I was going to get them all clean. This was it. I held my breath, unlocked the door and walked into my first kennel.

Each one was identical, about the size of a small garden shed. The front had metal bars that reached all the way from the floor to the ceiling. The sides were plastic panels up to about waist height, with metal bars that ran from the tops of the panels right up to the ceiling. The back of the kennel was a concrete wall painted green. Every kennel had a dog bed and blanket in the back and a water bowl at the front.

I lifted Sunny into his bed before sloshing my bucket of water and disinfectant around the floor. Jacky told me I had to scrub the bars and the panels as well as the floor, and once they were clean I swept all the poo out of the kennel and into the drain just outside. Sunny watched from the safety of his dry bed as though he were aboard a boat in the middle of the sea!

'How am I doing, boy?' I asked him and he jumped out of the bed and trotted over to me, wagging his tail. I guessed this meant I was doing OK. I picked him up and we had a cuddle right then and there. Some things just cannot wait!

As I cleaned out the kennel, I was aware of two brown eyes watching me. A golden head with a grey face had popped up from the kennel next door and was looking at me with big seal-cub eyes.

'Hello. Who are you?' I heard myself ask as though expecting a reply.

She gave me a concerned squeak as if to say, 'When are you coming over to me?'

'Hang on; I'll be with you in a minute,' I reassured her.

Once Sunny's kennel was shining like a new pin, I patted him on the head and went next door to clean out his neighbour. Before I entered her kennel I read her card, clipped to the outside.

As well as the usual necessary information, it read: *loves a cuddle*. Well, that made two of us.

She was a stray, part golden retriever, part mongrel, quite elderly and was sitting down, wagging her tail at me. I wondered what her name could be and tried one out for luck.

'Goldie?'

She looked back at me with a blank expression. 'No? Oh well, Goldie will have to do for the time being,' I said, bending down to her level to give her a pat. She leaned back, balancing on her hind legs as if begging, then she burrowed her soft snout under my chin, put a paw either side of my neck and gave me a big hug! That was it: just like that, she'd stolen my heart.

She must have been house trained as her kennel was spotless and needed more of a dusting than a full spring-clean. Only a few were as clean as this one and most, especially the ones with two or three dogs in them, were much harder work. I didn't mind though, because every kennel I went into, the dogs greeted me with boundless love and enthusiasm.

By this time, Jacky had cleaned out half of her fifty kennels and I'd only cleaned out two! I'd better get cracking.

Once all the kennels were clean, it was time to feed our hundred hungry hounds. Jacky told me that when there was more than one dog in a kennel, I should stand in with them, placing the bowls at opposite ends. This would stop them fighting over the same bowl.

Hmm . . . easier said than done.

I put the two bowls down at *opposite* ends, but both dogs dived into the *same* one. They were eating as though they'd never seen food before, heads deep down in the bowl, but at the same time (and I'm not sure how) scrapping with each other. Food was flying everywhere!

I didn't know what to do. I looked around for

Jacky, but she was at the other end of the block, and with the noise of the trains and the barking she probably wouldn't have heard me anyway. No, I had to deal with this on my own.

I looked down at the two dogs.

'Sit!' I said in my sternest voice. 'Down! Heel?' They took no notice of me. They'd finished one bowl and were diving into the other, still fighting and eating at the same time. By the time both bowls were empty, they were covered in dog food and so was I! But there were still another ninety-eight hungry mouths to feed. How would I survive? Mostly by throwing the bowls down, shutting my eyes and hoping for the best!

There were so many dogs: everywhere I looked, everywhere I turned, and Battersea had rescued all of them. This was one of *the four Rs* in action and I was right in the middle of it! My block was only one of a dozen kennel blocks; there were five hundred kennels in total, all full-to-bursting with hounds. I was sad there were so many unwanted dogs, but I was glad to be there, helping as many as I could.

Once all the dogs were fed, it was time for *our* breakfast and I was starving. The staff area was full of other kennel maids also having their breakfast and, to my delight, there were about ten dogs up there too. As I tucked into my bacon and eggs, ten bums quickly gathered around me in a display of very best sits. Long drops of drool dribbled from their hopeful mouths and twenty eyes followed each forkful from the plate to my mouth and back again.

'Hey,' I said, 'you've had yours, this is mine!'

During breakfast, Jacky told me I'd done well. Wow; I'd never heard this kind of praise at school. I was in my element and loving every minute. I hadn't done well enough at school to become a vet, but this was an excellent alternate choice.

Jacky and I spent the time between breakfast and lunch washing up food bowls, filling water bowls, cleaning out the kennels and just being with the dogs. Every bit of it was fantastic, but best of all I loved going into kennels where there were three or four dogs all in together. As soon as you approached the kennel they'd be up on their back legs, clamouring for attention. Sometimes they'd climb on top of each other to gain an extra little bit of height. Once you were in the kennel, they'd be all over you – sniffing noses, jumping-up paws, waggy tails and licking tongues greeting you from every direction.

The dogs had large exercise yards outside where they could play and run around. Jacky expertly took eight youngsters outside and put them in one large yard together. They all had wonderful saggy, baggy, wrinkled skin and huge paws. We couldn't help laughing as we watched them bound about, bumping into each other and falling on their faces. They were having the time of their lives! Dogs love the company of other dogs, just like people love the company of other people.

The kennel block that Jacky and I looked after housed the stray dogs. I suspected most of them had been dumped by owners that didn't want them any more, but I hoped some nicer owners would come in to see if their lost dogs were here.

A few people trudged through. Some had expectant looks on their faces, some angry faces, and others just looked really worried.

One of the worried faces belonged to a lady wearing a long skirt, ankle boots, a reddish jacket and a flowery hat. She was carrying a large bag and an umbrella and looked just like Mary Poppins.

'She's never run off before,' the lady said to me, a little teary-eyed. 'I just hope she's here. I couldn't bear the thought that she's roaming the streets all confused, frightened and alone.'

Halfway down the block she found her dog. It was my friend, Goldie!

'Tulip!' she cried, throwing her arms in the air. 'Where have you been?' No wonder the dog wouldn't answer to 'Goldie'. Tulip let out a squeal of joy when she saw her owner.

I found out that Tulip was ten years old, which is quite old in dog years because one dog year is the same as seven human years. This meant that if Tulip were human, she'd be seventy! That explained the grey face, because just like people, dogs go grey when they get old.

Tulip had been on the same walk every day since she was a puppy – through the park gate, once round the duck pond, down to the woods and ending up at the café where she and her owner would have a cup of tea each and share a sticky bun. Yesterday, however, Tulip had decided it was time for a little adventure. Just after the duck pond, she had run out of the park and boarded the number 159 bus. Her owner had watched in horror, but was too far away to catch the bus. The driver didn't hear her shrieks; he hadn't even noticed that Tulip had got on his bus at all!

Tulip ended up in the heart of busy, bustling

London and was brought into Battersea Dogs Home by a kindly dog-lover. Thank goodness – she could have been run over if he hadn't, but instead, here Goldie was being reunited with her owner and I was seeing Battersea's second *R* in action.

I opened the kennel door to let Tulip's owner in and you can guess what happened. Tulip gave her a big hug! I watched them happily trot away together, thinking this meant one less kennel to attend to. But before I knew it, an enormous black, rather sad-looking dog had taken Tulip's place.

CHAPTER FOUR

Roscoe's Disappearing Hat

'AAAAWWWOOOOOOOO!' wailed the sad-looking black dog, howling for all he was worth.

His head was tipped right back so that his big, long ears flopped down his neck and his nose pointed straight up to the ceiling. At the end of his howl, his lips came together as though he was about to blow out a candle.

His name was Roscoe and he was a one-year-old part Labrador, part German shepherd.

Roscoe had lived with his master all his life, but his master had just died, leaving Roscoe all alone in the world. No wonder he was sad. He needed cheering up and I knew just how to do it. Or so I thought.

I tried everything I could think of to make him feel better. I took him for walks, threw a tennis ball for him, squeaked a squeaky slipper for him and even bought him sausages from the canteen, but nothing worked.

'Come on, Roscoe,' I said, stroking his huge black head. 'Cheer up, boy.' But he just lay in his bed with his chin on the floor.

Every time someone came into the kennel block, Roscoe would lift his head up, but when he saw it wasn't his master, he'd either let out a big sigh and put his chin back down on the floor again or begin one of his record-breaking howls. I felt very sorry for him and racked my brains to try and find a way to help him feel a little happier.

Just then, Jacky came rushing into the block.

'Quick,' she said, out of breath. 'Have you seen a hat?'

'Pardon?' I said, confused.

'Roscoe had his master's hat with him when he came into Battersea,' she said. 'It was like his security blanket. Poor dog can't have his owner back, so his hat is the next best thing. If anything is going to cheer Roscoe up, it'll be that. Have you seen it?'

'No,' I said. So Jacky and I began a search of the whole of the dogs home. As you can imagine, it took a long time to search five hundred kennels. Most of the dogs were at the front of their kennels so it was easy to peek in and see if the hat was there, but if there were a lot of toys, blankets or dogs in a kennel, we had to go in for a proper look.

'Excuse me,' I said to a rather startled-looking spaniel as I lifted her up and looked underneath her.

'I'm terribly sorry to disturb you,' I said to a pair of poodles I had to part.

I didn't bother checking underneath the Chihuahuas; after all, being the world's smallest breed, the hat would have been bigger than them!

We also checked the vans that brought the dogs into Battersea, the canteen, the dogs' exercise yards and all the offices where the office staff worked. Eventually we found the hat in the veterinary department where the sick dogs go to get better.

I'm not quite sure what it was doing there, but Jacky grabbed it and we rushed back to our kennel block. I reached Roscoe's kennel first and he lifted up his head. When he saw I wasn't his beloved master, his chin hit the floor again. But a second later it was up again and he was sniffing the air – Jacky had just entered the kennel block with the hat.

A dog can smell hundreds of times better than we can and relies on its nose much more than its eyes and ears. We use our eyes to gather information about what is happening around us, but dogs mostly use their noses. In fact, we have about five million scent-detecting cells in our nose whereas a German shepherd has 225 million. This means that if someone touched just one grain of sand on a whole beach, their dog would be able to find that one grain of sand!

Roscoe smelled the hat before he saw it, and by the time Jacky reached his kennel he was out of his bed and up on his feet doing a sort of dance. We unlocked the door as quickly as we could and placed the hat in front of Roscoe.

His tail was now upright and for the first time it began madly wagging, thumping against the wall. His nose was all over the hat, sniffing it so wildly that it was scooting across the kennel floor in every direction, including right up in the air! Roscoe's hard-working nose was flipping it all over the place. Finally the dog began to settle down. He plodded over to his bed where he laid down with his master's hat between his two front paws, gently resting his head on its brown felt top.

Now Roscoe was much happier, he and his hat could move to the rehoming kennel block where he would hopefully find a new home soon.

Until I came to Battersea Dogs Home, I didn't know much about dogs. I thought I did – I'd read lots of books about them – but there was nothing like having hands-on experience. I was learning all sorts of brilliant new things and when Jacky taught me how to tell how old a dog is, I felt like the cleverest person in the whole world.

'Right,' she said. 'The best way to tell a dog's age is is by looking at its teeth.' At the end of Jacky's lead were two dogs: a fat, elderly mongrel and a lively, young terrier. The old girl was panting – her long pink tongue hung from the side of her mouth and she was drooling all over the place. Her breath smelled of rotten eggs, but she had a twinkle in her eyes and a waggy tail. The youngster was jumping around as though he had ants in his pants, eager to be let off the lead.

Jacky kneeled down next to the terrier and carefully pulled his lips up so that we could see his teeth.

'Anything under five months old will have needle-like puppy teeth. Watch your fingers on those!' she advised me. She was right: the terrier's teeth were bright white, but thin and needle-sharp. His gums were perfect, candyfloss pink.

'At about five or six months the dog loses its baby teeth in the same way we do when we're about six or seven years old,' she said. 'If the dog has all its adult teeth, but they are still nice and white and its gums nice and pink, the dog is probably between five and twelve months old.'

Right, I thought. I could remember that.

'If the teeth are starting to turn brown and showing signs of wearing down, the dog is usually approaching middle age – about six or seven.' Jacky then pulled the fat mongrel's chops right up and back so that I could see all her pearly whites – which were anything but pearly white.

'Her gums aren't so pink any more and see how her back teeth have worn right down? Even her front teeth aren't too good,' she said.

I peered into the mongrel's mouth, which was extremely whiffy. Her teeth were shocking: all brown and cracked, and they were no longer pointed, but flat. Slobber dripped from her jowls.

'This one's probably a stone-chewer, which is why her teeth are so flat,' Jacky pointed out. 'Going by her teeth, I'd say she's about ten years old.' I'm not sure if the dog was protesting at this, but just at that moment she shook her head and covered us both in stinky drool.

'OK, I've lined up a few friendly hounds to test you on,' she said, bringing out five new dogs, one after the other. I was a little nervous, not of the dogs, just that I might fail. But I concentrated hard and tried to remember everything Jacky had shown me, and to my surprise and delight I got every single one right!

I may have left school, but my education was far from over.

After a few weeks at Battersea Dogs Home, I could not only tell a dog's age, but I was also much better (and quicker!) at cleaning out and feeding the dogs too. In fact, I hardly got any poo or dog food on me any more. I could walk one dog at a time quite easily now, but still had trouble walking two or three. Jacky thought it was time I got the hang of it.

'OK,' she said, 'watch closely.'

I watched as she confidently walked into a kennel, pushed three large, leaping dogs down, told them in a loud voice to sit and expertly clipped their leads on with no fuss at all. She walked them down to the end of the kennel block and waited for me.

I swallowed hard. My hands were shaking as I fed the key into the lock. The three dogs in my kennel were turning somersaults with excitement and a wrestling match began as I tried to clip three leads onto three collars whilst in the middle of a tangle of . . .

twelve paws,

six ears,

three tails,

three noses,

and three tongues.

In amongst all of this, how was I supposed to find the three tiny metal rings on which to hook my trembling leads?

As I found out for myself, taking more than one dog out at a time is something only very experienced kennel maids should try.

The first dog, a shaggy tan-coloured mongrel, shot through my legs like a rocket. I whizzed round and began chasing it, but had forgotten to close the kennel door on the other two and as I sped down the kennel block trying to catch the first, the other two overtook me. Jacky was at the other end of the block, holding her three dogs, and watched in horror as three more (plus me) came hurtling towards her. She managed to catch two of them, but the third shot past her and ran out the door.

Thankfully he didn't get too far and I was relieved to see someone grab hold of him. When I realized who it was, I turned a bright shade of red.

'Hello there!' Mr Wadman Taylor called to me, between puffs on his pipe. He patted the shaggy brown dog who was now sitting obediently at his feet. 'How are you getting on?' he asked, stroking his white beard. He reminded me of Father Christmas, only not as fat.

'Erm, fine thanks,' I said, rather embarrassed, and so red by now that I looked just like a strawberry. I clipped my lead onto the dog's collar and hurried back to Jacky, who was struggling to control five dogs.

I tried to take control of my three hounds as best I could and we began our walk. Their tongues were hanging out and their eyeballs were almost popping out of their heads. I was being dragged all over the place, and by the time we returned to the kennel block I felt like both my arms were longer than when we started out!

I'd only just recovered from that wild walk when Jacky told me it was time for my next lesson – bathing a dog. Most of them looked (and smelled) like they needed a bath, but which one of these mucky pups would I choose? I didn't need to worry, because he chose me . . .

CHAPTER FIVE

Pepe Le Pew's Spectacular Stink

He was sitting at the back of his kennel, shaking like a jelly on a train.

The noise in our kennel block was nearly deafening, each of our hundred dogs shouting louder than the others, trying to be heard.

'QUIET!' I yelled, and to my surprise they all stopped.

He was a new arrival and had only come in the day before. I unlocked the kennel door and slowly walked in. The terrified little Border collie squeezed himself as far back against the wall as he possibly could. He was mostly black with short hair, except for a few longer tufts that sprouted out here and there. He had a muddy white stripe running from the top of his head right down to his snout. His chest and two front paws were also off-white, like grimy old sports socks you'd find at the bottom of your gym bag.

When I was near him, but not close enough to scare him, I kneeled down to his level. I tried to make myself as small as I could so that I didn't frighten him any more than he already was. He had stopped shaking, but his eyes were large and round with fear and he never took them off me. The other dogs started barking again.

I knew that looking right into his eyes might worry him so I looked down at his chest while I pulled a roast-beef-flavoured Schmacko from my pocket. I held out my hand and he leaned forward, his nose sniffing the air. He gently took the treat, but kept a watchful eye on me. I offered him another, which he took, and then another. This dog loved roast beef!

I remembered what Jacky had told me on my first day and didn't try to pat him on his head in case he thought I was going to hit him. Instead, I leaned forward and stroked his chest, which he didn't seem to mind. As I got closer to him, I was nearly knocked out by his smell! It was worse than old pants and smelled as though he'd rolled in foxes' poo, or worse. He didn't seem to notice the smell, or if he did, it didn't worry him.

'*Pee-ew!*' I said. 'I'm going to call you Pepe Le Pew, after the stinky cartoon skunk.' To my delight, the end of his tail wagged ever so slightly – he must have liked his new name.

Pepe Le Pew had a bad case of kennel cough, which is a bit like human flu. At that moment he sneezed and a huge blob of snot shot out of his nose and hit me right in the eye. Not wanting to make any sudden movements and scare him,

I slowly raised my arm to my face and wiped it clear with my sleeve. Luckily doggy flu isn't contagious to humans!

'Well, thanks for that, boy,' I said to him and his tail wagged a little more; it was almost as though he was laughing at me. I left him with two more Schmackos and promised to visit him the very next day.

At my job interview, Mr Wadman Taylor had told me that some dogs come into Battersea Dogs Home very frightened. Pepe was definitely one of those dogs. As well as having been rescued by Battersea, Pepe was in desperate need of another of *the four Rs* – rehabilitation.

Mr Wadman Taylor had explained that a dog could be nervous because its last owner hadn't treated it well, but it could also be nervous if it was never properly socialized. Imagine if you lived in a cupboard for the first seven years of your life – and then one day you came out. You'd be very under-socialized, and as a result scared of all the strange sights and sounds around you. If you'd never seen them before, things like traffic, other children, animals, television, bicycles, aeroplanes and everything else would terrify you. And so dogs that haven't been shown what's out there in the world can also be very nervous. The most important time to show dogs as much as possible is when they are puppies so that they can get used to everything straightaway.

Mr Wadman Taylor had told me that to properly socialize a nervous dog, I had to build up a bond by spending regular time with it. It was important for me to take it slowly though: not to rush the dog, rather let it relax and start to trust me when it was ready, not when I was!

'It might take a while,' he said to me, 'but once they trust you, they'll always trust you and you'll have a friend for life.'

I spent time with Pepe Le Pew every day and took him out for walks to get him used to everything. I don't think his last owner could have been very nice to him because it took quite a long time for him to trust me and relax. Whenever I arrived at his kennel he would be at the back, shaking, but with every passing day Pepe became happier and friendlier.

On the fifth day he was right at the front of the kennel, up on his two back legs waiting for me. He was doing a sort of wiggle from left to right, wagging his tail and straining to see if it was me. When he saw it *was* me walking up to his kennel, he let out a half-howl, half-squeal of delight as if to say, 'Where have you been? I've been waiting ages. I could really do with one of those roast-beef Schmackos. Let's go walkies, come on, hurry up, *let's go!*'

'OK, OK,' I said. 'Calm down!' I unlocked the kennel door and bent down to him. I pulled out my lead and tried to clip it onto his collar.

Pepe was so excited he was jumping all over the place like a kangaroo and I couldn't clip the lead onto the small metal ring on his collar.

'Settle down!' I said, but it didn't do any good, and as I was fumbling with the collar and lead, Pepe Le Pew managed to wriggle free. I'd left the door open and he shot past me, straight out of the kennel block. Oh no, not again!

All the other dogs were in a frenzy, barking their heads off.

The Labrador in the kennel next door seemed to be saying, 'Look out, he's off!' *Yes, thank you, I can see that*, I thought to myself.

The posh-looking poodle opposite was saying, 'I say, do you know that dog's escaping?' Yes, I had noticed.

And the Scottie two doors down was barking intently after Pepe, as if to say, 'Run for your life, laddie, and don't look back!'

I raced down the block after Pepe. Thankfully he hadn't got far. Rather than running out the door, he saw (or probably smelled) the food in the kitchen and I found him with his head in a large bag of biscuits, happily chomping away. I clipped the lead to his collar and waited for a moment.

'Had enough?' I asked, looking down at

him with my eyebrows raised. With his mouth full of dog biscuits, he looked up at me and wagged his tail before shoving his head back in the bag and helping himself to seconds. After a few more biscuits, I gently pulled him away and he trotted contentedly beside me, eager for his walk to begin. He wouldn't have been so pleased if he had known where we were really going. We took a sharp left and I opened up the door to the grooming room.

Pepe was a lot happier now, but he still stunk of old pants, old socks, blue cheese and farts all rolled into one. It was time for me to rid him of his spectacular stink. The day before Jacky had shown me how to bathe a dog. It wasn't hard – it was a lot like bathing yourself and shampooing your hair. The trick was to stop the dog jumping out of the bath.

Jacky had picked a big, fat golden retriever who loved having a bath, was very well-behaved and didn't try to escape once. I hoped Pepe would be just as good for me.

As we entered the grooming room, an Old English sheepdog and its kennel maid were just leaving. The dog's hair was big and fluffy and standing on end. He looked like he'd stuck his paw in an electric socket!

The room was hot and humid from the dryer and there were clumps of hair all over the floor, just like at a hairdresser. In the room was a large bath with a shower attachment for washing dogs, a table and lots of cupboards and shelves containing grooming equipment. One long shelf was filled with dozens of different brushes. Some had spiky teeth for coarse-haired dogs like terriers, some had soft teeth for very smooth-haired dogs like whippets and others were just like human hairbrushes for dogs somewhere in between. Pepe nosed them all, sniffing out the grooming room's previous customers.

Poor thing. He thought he was just here for a brush. He hadn't realized he was going in the bath – but the moment I ran the taps, he knew what he was in for and bolted to the door.

'Sorry, boy,' I said to him. 'No escaping this time.'

When the water temperature was just right, I lifted Pepe Le Pew into the bath. He looked up at me with a mournful expression, as though this was the worst thing that had ever happened to him.

'Oh, come on, it's not that bad,' I said. 'Just think of how much better you'll smell.'

I moved the shower head slowly up and down the length of his body, thoroughly soaking his coat. Pepe was just about to do a monumental shake, which would have completely soaked me, but thanks to Jacky, I knew exactly how to deal with this. The fat golden retriever we'd bathed the day before had tried the same thing and I'd watched as Jacky had expertly stopped him in his tracks.

'When a dog starts to shake his coat out,' she'd said, 'just grab him by his scruff – the fatty skin around the top of his neck.'

It had worked with the retriever, but now

it was Pepe's turn and I wasn't as confident as Jacky. Just as he began his shake, I grabbed Pepe's scruff and the shake stopped in its tracks. It worked! What a brilliant trick, it was just like putting your finger under someone's nose to stop them sneezing.

The water flattened Pepe's tufty fur right against his skin and I could see that underneath, he was quite thin. His last owner obviously hadn't fed him enough. I gave him another roast-beef snack, which he gobbled up just like a Hoover running over a sock.

Pepe squirmed as the shower did its job and a stream of foul-smelling brown water flowed down the plughole. Next, I squirted half a handful of pink shampoo onto his back and began to massage it in. First I massaged his back, then his neck and when I reached his ears, he let out a contented moan. I actually think he was enjoying it! He'd stopped wriggling and was now looking up at me as though I was his all-time best friend.

'See,' I said to him with a smile, 'it's not so bad, is it? And you smell a hundred times better!'

I rinsed off all the soapsuds, and when the water draining from him was clear, I knew that not only was all the soap out, but also all the fox poo too.

The tricky bit was still to come. His doggy flu was much better, but I didn't want it to come back so I had to dry him under a big dog-sized hairdryer. It was as tall as me and quite heavy so it was on wheels. It had a long nozzle from where the hot air blew, which made it look like a baby elephant on roller skates! Most dogs hate the dryer even more than the bath and I was sure Pepe would be no different.

I lifted him gently onto the table and at first pointed the dryer away from him. Even so, he looked warily at its large trunk. I put it on low to see how he would react. He didn't seem too worried so I slowly moved the nozzle over to his bottom, as far away from his head as I could.

He jumped a little, but the air was warm and he seemed to like it. So far so good, but on the slow setting we'd be here all day. I turned it up to a faster level and Pepe squealed and leaped off the table.

'OK, boy,' I said reassuringly, 'we'll put it back on slow. I just hope you don't have to be anywhere this afternoon, this is going to take a while.'

An hour later Pepe was completely dry, extremely fluffy and smelled like strawberries. As we left the grooming room, he bumped into a German shepherd, which he tried to get away from as quickly as possible. I don't think he was frightened of the bigger dog – I think he was embarrassed to be looking (and smelling) like a large black-and-white poodle!

The next day I took Pepe to see the vet. We had to wait our turn because Mr Wadman Taylor was microchipping a pug who was just about to go off to her new home. Microchips are a type of identification. They're about the size of a grain of rice and are injected into the dog's scruff, which is quite fatty so the dog doesn't usually feel anything. It's a little like having an injection and the pug didn't seem to mind, especially as Mr Wadman Taylor gave her a roast beef-flavoured Schmacko afterwards.

The tiny microchip contained her owner's name, address and phone number electronically. If the pug were to get lost and turn up at a police station or a dog rescue centre like Battersea, a hand-held scanner would be waved over her neck and the microchip number would appear on the scanner. That number would then be typed into a computer, her owner's details would come up and they'd get a call telling them where their pug was!

Wearing a collar and tag is just as important, but sometimes dogs lose their collars so without a microchip there would be no way of knowing who a lost dog belonged to.

When the pug and her new owners had

left, Mr Wadman Taylor turned his attention to Pepe. Mr Wadman Taylor was very tall and wore a white coat. He was also puffing away on his pipe so Pepe might have mistaken him for a dragon!

'Who have we got here then?' he asked me.

'His name's Pepe Le Pew,' I said.

'After the stinky cartoon skunk?' Mr Wadman Taylor asked. 'That's funny. He smells lovely to me, just like strawberries!'

'Yes, he had a bath yesterday,' I explained.

Pepe wasn't sure about being friends with Mr Wadman Taylor at first. But when the man kneeled down, stroked Pepe on the chest and gave him a Schmacko, Pepe decided he was OK after all. I lifted Pepe onto the table.

Mr Wadman Taylor already had his stethoscope in his ears and he placed the other end onto Pepe's chest. He listened for a while to see if Pepe's cough had cleared up and then said, 'Well, my boy, you sound much better. I think it's time we found you a new home.'

Pepe seemed to like that idea and his tail madly thumped the table.

I wasn't sure if I liked it though. Pepe was my favourite dog and I knew that as soon as someone saw him, they'd pick him to be their pet. He was so handsome with his sleek black fur and his newly dazzling white fluffy bits. His brown eyes were the softest doggy eyes I'd ever seen and now that he smelled of strawberries, who could resist him?

I was right; only an hour after being put up for rehoming, Pepe Le Pew *was* chosen!

Battersea has a special team of people whose job it is to find the dogs new homes. They are called *rehomers* and wear red sweatshirts with the same picture of the dog that my blue sweatshirt had on it. They also wear black jeans and black shoes.

As Pepe Le Pew was led away to begin his new life, he got loose from his rehomer and ran back to me. He jumped straight into my arms and gave me one last lick.

'Go on, Pepe, off you go,' I said to him. 'Your new owners will love you and look after you.' He seemed to understand because he turned his head towards them and happily trotted back.

I watched him being rehomed and realized I was seeing another of Battersea's *four Rs*. I thought to myself that being a rehomer and helping the dogs find good new homes must be a wonderful job. I knew they often got letters and photos from nice families they had rehomed dogs to. The dogs always looked happy and well cared for in the pictures.

But I had something much better than a photo to look forward to – Pepe's new owners said that I could go and visit him any time I liked!

My very first days as a kennel maid

With Roscoe, my favourite Battersea dog

Battersea's historic past

An air-conditioned animal ambulance

A very unique pencil holder, Battersea style

Will you rescue me?

Benjamin, the mutt who met the Monarch

Battersea's Annual Reunion enjoyed by young, old and even canine superheroes

My office as rehoming manager

CHAPTER SIX

Benjamin Meets the Queen

Jacky came running into the kennel block at full speed. I'd just washed down the central aisle and it was all soapy, wet and slippery.

'*AAARRRRRGGGHHHH!*' she wailed as she slid half the length of the block, coming to a skidding halt on her bum and crashing into me. 'You'll never guess who's coming to Battersea Dogs Home?' she wheezed, out of breath.

'Who?' I said, untangling myself from her

and the broom I'd been using to sweep the aisle.

'I'll give you a clue,' she said, getting to her feet. 'She's a very important lady and she loves dogs.'

Well, it can't be my mum then, I thought to myself. 'Give me another clue,' I said.

'OK, her favourite dogs are corgis.' I still wasn't getting it. 'And her name is Elizabeth.'

'Oh my goodness,' I said, my eyes as big as Frisbees. 'The Queen! The Queen is coming here?'

In one week's time, the Queen was coming to visit us at Battersea Dogs Home. Everything – from windows to West Highland terriers – was washed. Door knobs, Dobermans and Dalmatians were all dusted down. Paintwork and poodles were painstakingly polished until everything was gleaming.

Jacky and I were told that the Queen might walk through our kennel block so it had to be especially shiny and clean.

Right then, my favourite dog was a cream-coloured lurcher called Benjamin. He had fuzzy fur, chocolate-brown eyes and ears that pointed upwards but flopped over at the tips. When the kennel block was all tidy and sparkling, I bathed Benjamin and tied a blue bow tie round his neck. My, he looked handsome!

Six staff, including Jacky and me, had been chosen to welcome the Queen. We were each allowed to have one dog with us. I wanted Benjamin, but Mr Wadman Taylor decided the dogs had to be staff dogs so that we knew for sure that they were super well-behaved. So six of the friendliest staff dogs were picked. Not having a dog of my own, I borrowed a dopey Labrador called Charles, who belonged to another kennel maid.

Five minutes before the Queen arrived, the six of us and our dogs took our places. Three minutes before the Queen arrived, Charles the Labrador squatted, did the biggest fart I'd ever heard and then squirted everything around him with foul-smelling, bright-yellow diarrhoea.

Everyone held their breath, not just because of the smell, but because the Queen was arriving in two and a half minutes!

There wasn't much time. Five kennel maids appeared from nowhere with buckets of water, disinfectant and brooms. The liquid poo was washed away in a matter of seconds and even the eggy stench began to waft away. I looked down at Charles who looked up at me. He seemed to be saying, 'There could be more where that came from!'

I suggested to Mr Wadman Taylor that we swap Charles for another dog.

'Have you got one in mind?' he asked me.

'Oh yes,' I said. 'His name's Benjamin.'

'Is he friendly?' he asked.

'Extremely,' I replied.

'Are you sure?' he asked, looking a little worried. 'The newspapers and television will have a field day if Benjamin bites the Queen.'

'I'm sure,' I said – well, as sure as I could be;

he'd always been lovely with me, anyway! So out Benjamin came in his blue bow tie, looking like he'd been born to meet the Queen.

Just then the royal car pulled up and the Queen stepped out. She was much smaller than I thought she'd be and looked just like my granny. She wore a lovely purple dress with matching hat, white shoes and was carrying a bunch of beautiful yellow flowers. As soon as she saw the six dogs, the Queen's face lit up and she smiled a smile that came straight from her heart.

Her gaze fell from one dog to the next until she had eyed all six. To my joy, she walked straight over to Benjamin and reached out to him. I could see Mr Wadman Taylor tense and hold his breath.

The Queen is a very experienced dog owner and a genuine dog-lover, and she approached Benjamin in exactly the right way; with the palm of her hand held out for him to sniff. She waited until he'd had a good sniff of her hand (even though she was wearing gloves) before stroking his chest affectionately and then working her way up to a scratch behind his ear.

I watched in wonderment as the Queen of England stroked this beautifully-behaved stray dog from the streets of London. As the Queen moved on, Mr Wadman Taylor winked at me and breathed a huge sigh of relief.

The next day the newspapers were full of pictures of the royal visit and the Queen stroking Benjamin. A lovely family whose elderly lurcher had recently died saw the pictures and drove for four hours from Devon that morning, in the hope they might have just the right home for Benjamin. They did, and although I missed him terribly when he left, I knew he was off to a better life, spending his days lying in front of an open farmhouse fire and going for long walks on the beach.

He is now a celebrity in his village; they call him 'the mutt that met the monarch.'

Pepe Le Pew's new owners had said I could visit him in his new home, and three months after waving him goodbye at Battersea Dogs Home, that's exactly what I did.

But I wasn't prepared for what awaited me.

I was so excited to be seeing my boy again I could barely sit still on the bus. I walked up to Mr and Mrs Hall's front door and rang the bell. Then came the first thing that was strange – from inside the house came an enormous and very deep bark.

'*WOOOOOOF. WOOOOOOOOOOOF, WOOOOOOOOOOOF.*'

It sounded more like a Rottweiler than a Border collie. Come to think of it, I'd never heard Pepe bark properly at the dogs home. He'd let out the odd squeal when he was pleased to see me, but that was about all.

I rang the doorbell again and the same sound boomed down the stairs. Had I got the right house? I checked my piece of paper – I had. All of a sudden I felt rather nervous.

Mrs Hall opened the door and gave me a big hug. 'Come on up! Pepe is dying to see you,' she said, letting me lead the way. I looked up and saw Pepe at the very top. He looked bigger from that angle.

'Pepe Le Pew!' I squealed with delight. By this time he was barking his head off, pleased to see me, or so I thought. I rushed up the stairs to him and put my hand out to stroke him.

And then he bit me!

'Ow!' I said, shocked. I wasn't expecting that sort of greeting. My hand began bleeding. Mr Hall took Pepe into the kitchen and shut the door. We all looked at each other, not knowing what to say or do, then we went into the living room and sat down. Mrs Hall cleaned up my wound and put a plaster on it.

'Why on earth did he do that?' they both asked me. 'We can't understand it. Ever since Pepe has been with us we've spoiled him rotten. We've let him do whatever he wants, eat whatever he wants and go wherever he wants. Look, we even bought him his own sofa!' they said, pointing towards a Pepe-sized sofa.

That was exactly the problem. Although Mr and Mrs Hall had been kind to Pepe, loved him, taken care of him and looked after him, they hadn't been teaching him right from wrong or showing him what he was and wasn't allowed to do. Pepe thought *he* was the one in charge, not them. When Mrs Hall had tried to get into bed the other night, Pepe had tried to bite her because, being the boss, he thought that he should have the most comfy bed in the house, not her!

'You have to take charge of him,' I said to them. 'Swap the sofa for a dog bed, otherwise Pepe will see himself as a human. Make sure he sees that you two are the bosses. Only feed him once you've eaten, make him sit at the kerb when you take him for walks and whatever you do, don't let him get on any of the furniture. Furniture is for humans, not dogs. Be kind to him, but let him know that he is a dog – not a human.'

They both listened intently and nodded.

'It's for the best,' I said. 'Otherwise he'll bite someone and end up back at Battersea Dogs Home.'

I pulled out some of the roast-beef Schmackos that Pepe loved so much and asked Mr Hall to let him out of the kitchen. He came trotting into the living room as though nothing had happened. I showed him the Schmackos. He licked his lips.

'Pepe, sit!' I said in my sternest voice. He thought for a moment and decided to test me out, refusing to sit. '*Sit!*' I said again, this time a little louder. He immediately sat, so I gave him the treat. 'Give me your paw,' I said. He wouldn't.

I explained to Mr and Mrs Hall that if you give a dog a command and he doesn't do it, you should ask him again until he does, otherwise he mustn't be given the treat.

'Give me your paw,' I said again. He nosed the Schmacko. 'You're not getting it until you've given me your paw. I know you know how to, Pepe; after all, it was me who taught you! Give paw,' I asked for the third time. He gave me his paw and I gave him the Schmacko. He licked my ear. We were friends again and even had a cuddle – on the floor, not on the sofa!

A few months later I visited Pepe again. His reaction this time was much more what I was hoping for. He had, of course, remembered me and came bounding over, threw himself into my arms and frantically licked my face.

Mr and Mrs Hall had done exactly what I had advised and now Pepe was a whole lot happier and behaving far better. Mr and Mrs Hall were much happier too – and the best news of all, there wasn't a dog sofa in sight!

The next day at Battersea I cleaned out and fed all of my fifty dogs in record-breaking time (almost beating Jacky!). I also walked four dogs at once without losing any of them, bathed and groomed three dogs one after the other without once getting splashed and I socialized four nervous dogs who, by the time I'd finished with them, were all wagging their tails!

I'd definitely mastered all the duties of a kennel maid, and when I saw how happy Pepe Le Pew now was in his new home, I wondered if I should try my hand at rehoming. I imagined it must be wonderful and very rewarding to help the dogs find new homes. This was a tough decision though, because I knew it would mean spending less time with the dogs and more time with Battersea's human customers.

Hmm, what would you have done?

CHAPTER SEVEN

Buster Busts a Move

Mr and Mrs Hall had given me a photo of Pepe. I stuck it on the front of my locker at Battersea, which meant I saw his happy face beaming back at me several times a day.

Knowing he was so contented in his new home gave me the same feeling as eating hot buttered toast on a cold, rainy day. It made me feel all warm inside, and knowing his happiness was made possible by the rehoming team, I decided I now wanted to become a rehomer.

I said farewell to Jacky and all the dogs in our kennel block (promising I'd come back to visit them), and made my way over to the rehoming section. It was a smart building that housed about two hundred dogs. It also had plenty of human areas, including a reception where people who wanted to rehome a dog patiently waited.

Mickey, the head rehomer, was also waiting patiently – for me.

'Well, hello there,' she said. Mickey was tall with curly hair and wore lots of rings on her fingers. 'So you want to be a rehomer, then?'

'Oh yes,' I said. 'I really do!'

'Well,' she said to me, 'if you're going to be a rehomer, the first thing we have to do is give you some new clothes.'

'New clothes? What's wrong with the ones I've got?' I asked.

'Nothing, if you're a kennel maid, but rehomers wear red sweatshirts and black jeans,' Mickey said, handing over my brand-new uniform. I started to change my sweatshirt, but

Mickey held her hand up and shook her head. 'You can only wear it when you've passed your training,' she said.

I couldn't wait to get started!

'There are two parts to rehoming,' she explained. 'First is the interview.' And she showed me the form people had to fill in.

'It's very long,' I said, to which Mickey replied, 'There's a lot we need to know!'

I glanced over the form. There were lots of questions, including how big the person's house was, whether they had a garden and who would look after the dog during the day. There were questions asking if they had kids, other dogs or cats and also whether the person had had dogs before.

Mickey explained that it was the rehomer's job to go through the form with the customer and then ask some extra questions as well. If the rehomer thought the person could offer a Battersea dog a good home, the second part to the rehoming would begin.

'This is where we help customers to find the dog that's right for them, and this part can be just as tricky as the interview,' she said. 'For example, you wouldn't give a large, boisterous young dog to an elderly person because they wouldn't be able to cope with it or even handle it.' That made sense, I thought, as I pictured my granny trying to control a nutty Great Dane! 'And you wouldn't give a snappy dog to a family with children,' she continued. 'Or a dog that howls when it is left alone to someone who is out for some of the day.'

This all made perfect sense to me and I couldn't wait to have a go. Mickey sat with me while I did my first interview in case I needed her help. A large black dog was also in the interview room, watching over proceedings.

On closer inspection, I saw that it wasn't just any old large black dog. From the hat he was holding in his mouth, I could tell it was Roscoe!

'Hello, boy!' I said, scratching his right ear.

'What are you doing in here?' He didn't answer; instead, he jumped up so that his two front paws were on my shoulders and he wagged his tail as hard as he could.

Mickey answered for him. 'Sometimes we bring dogs into the interview rooms to help them find a new owner,' she said. 'You see, when people look around the kennels and look at so many dogs, they find it hard just to choose one. Sometimes they'll pick the first they see, which is often the dog in the interview room.'

What a brilliant idea, I thought to myself!

A couple called James and Sarah came into my interview room and sat down. They were very nice and I liked them straightaway. James was tall with dark hair and a moustache, and he wore round gold-rimmed glasses. Sarah had long blonde hair, blue eyes and a very pretty dress with colourful flowers on it.

Roscoe seemed to like them too. He wandered over to James and plonked the hat right in his lap! I'd never seen him do that before – he was so attached to it that he carried it in his mouth at all times (except when he was eating, of course).

They sat stroking Roscoe while I asked them some questions.

They lived in the country in a large house with a garden. They had had a big dog before called Sheba, but she had grown old and had died a few weeks before. James and Sarah were very upset by this and were now hoping to give a home to a dog that didn't have one. They wanted a large dog that was friendly and liked going for walks. That sounded just like Roscoe!

'Is he available?' James asked.

'Oh, yes,' I said, 'and he seems to like you. I've never seen him give anyone his hat before!'

Just then, Roscoe jumped up onto James's lap – almost causing his chair to fall backwards – and gave him a big, wet, sloppy kiss that started from the bottom of James's chin and went right up over his nose, eyes and forehead, all the way to the top of his head!

'I think *he's* chosen *us*!' Sarah said. 'Can we take him home?'

I had gone through their form and asked them all the questions I needed to. I was convinced they were good owners and, more importantly, the right owners for Roscoe. I looked at Mickey to make sure she thought so too. She nodded.

'I think you've got yourself a new dog,' I said to James and Sarah. And turning to Roscoe, I said, 'And I think you've found yourself a new home, boy!'

While James, Sarah and Roscoe were in Battersea's shop buying a dog bed and a new collar and lead, I rushed to find Jacky.

'He's going!' I said, out of breath from running all the way to the other end of the kennel block. I'd made all the dogs start barking and it was hard to hear.

'What?' said Jacky.

'Roscoe. I've just rehomed him – he's going home!' I yelled over the din of the dogs.

Jacky squealed with delight and we both ran up to the shop to say goodbye.

'We promise we'll write and send photos,' James said.

'Oh, please do, we'll miss him so much,' I said.

Mickey, Jacky and I watched as the three of them walked away. Suddenly I noticed something was wrong.

'Hey, where's Roscoe's hat? He's forgotten it, we'll have to go and find it! *Stop them!*' I yelled to Jacky, turning round and racing back towards the interview room.

'Wait!' Jacky shouted after me. 'Look! It's there!'

'Where?' I couldn't see it, but I was looking in the wrong place. I was looking at Roscoe.

'There,' Jacky said, pointing at James. I looked over to the man who was walking along, proudly wearing the hat, with Roscoe looking lovingly up at him.

★

I didn't have time to miss Roscoe too much. My next challenge was to try and rehome Buster, a naughty two-year-old black-white-and-brown Jack Russell terrier. I knew it wouldn't be easy.

Rebecca, Mr Wadman Taylor's secretary, had told me all about Buster. He'd been put in her office because he had a poorly paw and wasn't allowed to get it wet so he couldn't stay in his kennel.

Rebecca had been on the phone when she suddenly realized Buster had escaped from her office. He was tearing down the stairs towards Poppy, Battersea's office cat. Hearing the screams a few seconds later, Rebecca dropped the phone and ran towards where they were coming from.

'Buster! Buster! Where are you?' she wailed after him.

She followed the trail of destruction Buster had left in his wake, terrified of what she might find. She imagined a tangle of paws and teeth, and tabby fur flying everywhere – poor Poppy!

But when Rebecca finally reached the rumpus, she found Buster lying on his back, four paws in the air, with a terrified look on his face. The screams had come from him! Poppy was standing over him, ears back, one paw on his chest, claws out.

Buster didn't realize that Poppy wasn't like most cats. She had come into Battersea as a kitten five years earlier. Battersea Dogs Home was all she had ever known and she strutted around like she owned the place. Most of the staff (including Rebecca and me) were terrified of her. She liked to snooze on top of the photocopier, daring anyone to come and use it. As for dogs, I'd never seen one get the better of her.

Rebecca rescued Buster from Poppy's claws and brought him back to her office.

'Oh my goodness,' she said to him, dabbing his nose with a tissue. Poppy had scratched his hooter and blood was dripping down it. 'What am I going to do with you?' He looked up at her with a sorry face and whimpered a little before licking her, which made her giggle uncontrollably.

Rebecca had taken a shine to this hooligan hound and had spoiled him rotten. But Buster was a bit like Pepe — and spoiling him was the worst thing she could possibly have done.

Buster had come into Battersea for never doing as he was told, fighting with the other dog in his house and chewing almost everything up. He'd eaten slippers, remote controls, chair and table legs, sunglasses, the sofa — even the wall!

Buster was naughty from the top of his nose right down to the tip of his tail and he needed some very special training. He was packed off to spend some time with the rehabilitation team.

The rehabilitation team at Battersea not only spent a lot of time socializing very nervous dogs, but they also taught dogs how to behave properly. If their owners had only done this when they were puppies, the dogs wouldn't now be crazy, naughty adults. It's easy to train a puppy, but when they get a bit older and naughtier, it can be a lot trickier.

Buster had been with the rehabilitation team for three days now and they were making good progress with him, but on his fourth day with them he was stolen from his kennel! Someone forced the lock and smuggled him out of the Home.

When Rebecca heard the terrible news, she spent the whole day sobbing. She was terribly worried about what might have happened to Buster. Three days went by with no news. Then on the fourth day, a dog fitting Buster's description was brought into Battersea by a member of the public. Rebecca raced down to see if it was him. She flung open the doors and there was Buster, looking a bit bedraggled and muddy but none the worse for his adventure. When he saw Rebecca, Buster let out a howl of delight and threw himself at her.

'Where did you get him from?' Rebecca asked the man, rather suspicious that he might have been the one who'd stolen Buster from Battersea.

'A man in the pub sold him to me,' he said. 'Fifty pounds he cost, but he's the worst-behaved dog in the whole world. He chewed my house and beat up a dog in the park,' he continued angrily. 'I don't even care about the fifty quid, just take him!' And with that, the man was gone.

We decided that whoever had pinched Buster in the first place had got more than they bargained for. Buster probably ate their home as well and if they had a cat, chances are he would have tried to snack on that too!

There was only one place Buster was going – back to rehab!

Buster's training continued and after two weeks he was like a different dog. All he needed was the same firm-but-kind training that Pepe Le Pew had needed. The rehabilitation team had also taught Buster to behave better around other animals.

Poppy was brought in to help Buster learn that cats were not put on this earth for him to chase. She taught him that cats have sharp claws and therefore should be respected, not chased!

Buster was also taken for walks with older, bigger dogs, and if he tried to start any trouble with them, they'd give him a doggy telling-off!

Before long, Buster was the best-behaved dog at Battersea Dogs Home and was ready to find a new home. The rehabilitation team had done their bit and now it was my turn. I found him a home at the seaside. His new owners had had naughty terriers before, so they knew what they were letting themselves in for just in case he went back to being the old Buster. They even had a cat that was used to dogs and sounded a bit like Poppy!

A month later it felt like my birthday. I received two cards in the Battersea post on the same day. One was from Buster's new owners and contained a photo of him sitting next to a large silver cup looking very pleased with himself – he'd won first prize at a local dog show for being the best-trained dog.

The other photo was of a large black dog, snoozing under a big oak tree, with a hat on his head. Can you guess who it was?

CHAPTER EIGHT

Boss Bounces Back

'What on earth is this, Burt?' said the driver of a car to another man.

'It's a dog, Bill.'

'I know it's a dog, I can see that,' replied the driver angrily.

From the back seat of the car, a rather chubby, ill-looking Border collie was staring straight back at them.

'Well, we'll just have to get rid of it.'

And with that, the driver got out, opened

the back door, grabbed the dog by the scruff of his neck and flung him out of the car. The poor dog landed hard on his backside – luckily he had enough padding there to cushion his fall.

Ten minutes earlier the Border collie had been snoring contentedly on the back seat of his family's car when all of a sudden the two men had flung open the doors, jumped in and fired up the engine. The car burst into life and, with wheels spinning and tyres smoking, it sped off like a racing car at the start of a race. Nought to sixty miles per hour in what seemed like just a few seconds.

The men hadn't noticed the collie on the back seat, and as they swerved the car from left to right, the poor dog was flung around in all directions. Whenever they turned a corner he was thrown against the doors and when they hit the brakes, he shot forward, ending up in a heap on the floor.

Now the collie was feeling very queasy; he'd

only just had his breakfast and it wasn't long before he was sick all over the back seat and all over himself. Then with one final violent chuck, he threw up all over the men in the front seats. The car screeched to a halt and that was when the men turned around to find they'd stolen more than they bargained for!

The Border collie now sat on the side of the road and watched as the car sped off. He looked all around him, but didn't recognize anything. He seemed to be in the middle of nowhere. There were no houses or people, no shops or traffic, just green fields and some woods in the distance. It was pouring with rain.

He was terrified, and in his panic ran over to the woods. He sheltered there until day turned to night and light turned to dark. He was soaking wet and shivering with cold. He dug a hole underneath a bush and burrowed in. Petrified by all the unfamiliar sounds, he didn't sleep a wink that night.

★

I'd just finished rehoming a rather wriggly little Border terrier puppy when Tony the dog warden strolled over to me. I remembered Mr Wadman Taylor telling me all about dog wardens. Their job was to educate people about responsible dog ownership, round up stray dogs found on their patch and make sure people scooped their dog's poop.

I liked Tony. He was short, round and friendly and had big bushy eyebrows just like a schnauzer.

'Hi, Tony, how are you?' I asked.

'I'm all right, thanks, but there's a Border collie on my patch that isn't. I've been trying to catch him for weeks now, but something or someone must have really spooked him,' he said. 'Every time I get anywhere near him, he scarpers, and he's so fast I've named him Quick!' Tony told me all the ingenious ways he'd tried to catch Quick, but with no luck. 'I'm just so worried about him, because he's losing weight and it looks like he's in a bad way.'

Tony had gone to great lengths to try and catch the poor dog. One attempt involved him building a large wooden box about the size of a washing machine, which he'd taken into the woods. He'd used a long stick to prop the box up and then tied string around the bottom of the stick. He trailed the string all the way back to a bush about twenty paces away. He had then covered the box with leaves, bracken and branches and did the same with the trail of string so that everything was camouflaged. Finally, he had placed four peanut butter sandwiches underneath the box, hidden behind the bush and waited. And waited. And waited.

Tony looked through his binoculars at the surrounding fields. He saw trees, wooden gates, hedges and endless green grass, but there was no sign of Quick so he decided to rest his eyes for a bit. He closed them for what he thought was only a minute or two. He woke himself up with his own snoring, which made him jump.

Tony looked at his watch and realized he'd been asleep for thirty minutes!

He spun over onto his front and looked intently towards the box. Directly beneath it was Quick, wolfing down the last peanut butter sandwich. Tony fumbled around in the leaves looking for the end of the string. When he finally found it, he yanked it hard. The stick at the other end of the string gave way and the box came tumbling down. *Thud!*

Quick, who by then had finished eating Tony's lunch, was already trotting away when he turned to see the box fall. He wasn't really sure what was going on and he didn't hang about to find out.

'He doesn't realize I just want to help him,' Tony said to me. 'If I could only catch him I could bring him in here to Battersea Dogs Home. I know the kennel maids would feed him up and then you could rehome him.' Tony knew Quick was a clever dog, but couldn't help thinking how silly he was at the same time.

He'd be much safer if he'd just let Tony catch him.

I felt so sorry for Quick and thought of Roscoe, Pepe Le Pew and Buster, all happy in their new homes, lying by the fire, warm, dry and loved. Poor Quick was out there all alone, probably cold, wet and starving, but what could Tony do if Quick didn't want to be caught?

Then one day, after three months of failed attempts, I received a phone call from a very excited Tony.

'I've got him! I've got him! He's in the back of my van. I'm coming in,' he wheezed down the phone.

When Tony arrived at Battersea I was waiting there to greet him and the famous Quick.

'So how did you do it?' I asked. 'Which one of your schemes got the better of him?'

'You won't believe it. I was having my lunch, sitting on the ledge at the back of my van, when Quick just appeared from nowhere, jumped up next to me, took my sandwich out of my hand

and wolfed it down! I offered him a bite of my Kit Kat too, which he nearly bit my hand off for. I took it really slowly, no sudden movements, sort of like I had a bucket full of slimy goo on my head that I didn't want to spill, and I held out my hand to stroke him. And he let me! I reckon old Quick had had enough of the open road.'

I peered into the back of the van and wasn't at all surprised. Looking back at me was a thin, raggedy, exhausted-looking dog with matted fur. His claws were overgrown, his head was bony and his front left paw was bleeding.

He was hungry and tired; dog-tired. He was tired from lack of sleep and from always being scared – but most of all, he was tired from running. He'd been running for so long.

I took him straight to Jacky who put him in a warm kennel and gave him a blanket and some food. As he finished his last mouthful, Quick fell asleep.

Two days later Quick was still catching up

on his sleep. He woke only to eat and go to the toilet after which he flopped back into bed.

I was showing a lady who'd lost her dog around my old kennel block where the strays were housed. She'd lost her dog, Boss, three months ago and came into Battersea nearly every day to look for him. She knew that the longer he was missing, the smaller the chance was of finding him.

As we walked further up the block, the lady explained to me that her kids desperately wanted Boss back; they were missing him so much, but had nearly given up hope of ever seeing him again.

Suddenly the lady stopped outside a kennel. In the back was a pathetic-looking creature, shaking like a leaf and terribly underweight.

I held my breath. It was Quick.

I asked her if she thought this was Boss. She looked at the dog's card.

'No, he's too thin,' she murmured, 'and this one's name is Quick.'

I explained that Quick was just a name Tony had given him, and also gently reminded her that her dog had been gone for three months and would probably look a little different from how he had looked when she last saw him.

The lady kneeled down, put her hand to the bars and ever so softly said, 'Boss?'

Quick stopped shaking for a few moments, lifted his scruffy head up from the concrete floor and tilted it to one side.

'Boss?' she said again, this time a little louder, a little more sure.

Quick stood up, still hesitant, still unsure but much more alert than before. My heart was beating fast.

It only took a few moments for Quick to realize that this was his long-lost owner, but once he did he squealed with joy and threw himself at the kennel door. His tail was wagging furiously and he was scratching at the bars like mad. When she realized it was Boss, the lady screamed; she was shaking and sobbing. With trembling hands, I unlocked the kennel door so that neither had to spend another second apart.

She threw herself at Quick and he threw himself at her.

'Boss, where have you been? We've all been worried sick,' she wailed, wiping the tears from her eyes. 'It's all right, boy, you're safe now.' Still shaking, she just kept saying, 'I've found you. I've found you, boy.'

When she had calmed down a little, the lady told me how the family car had been stolen three months ago with Boss in the back. A week later the police had found the car, but there had been no sign of Boss.

I called Tony – he just had to see this.

'Where are you?' I asked, breathless.

'As it happens, I'm pulling up to your front door with a little King Charles spaniel.'

'Come to the strays block straightaway,' I said.

Tony pulled up just in time to see Boss and his owner leaving the kennel block.

'Quick!' he called out in surprise.

'His name is Boss,' I explained to Tony, 'and his family has just found him.'

'Fantastic! And Boss is a much better name. Don't you look happy, boy?' he said, bending down to stroke Boss, who recognized Tony immediately and gave him a big lick.

Tony said goodbye to Boss and his owner and I went with them to reception, where the rest of Boss's family were waiting.

As the door opened, they all looked up. For a moment, nobody moved – too amazed to realize that, after three months of searching, their missing family member had finally been found.

And then they were all over him, four kids and their dad, yelling and crying too. I looked at Boss, who was smiling the biggest dog smile I'd ever seen, and as Boss was reunited with his family, I too had a grin that reached from ear to ear.

CHAPTER NINE

My Dog Gus

When I was seven years old I made a wish: 'I wish that I had a dog.' And I repeated that same wish every single year.

I had waited a long time, but at long last I knew my wish was finally about to come true.

I had been at Battersea for many years by now, first as a kennel maid, then as a rehomer and now I had been promoted to Rehoming Manager. This meant I had my own office.

I had also moved out of my parents' house

and was living in my own place. I knew I could take a dog to work with me, which meant it never had to stay at home on its own. And I had enough knowledge and experience to be able to train my new dog properly.

From having rehomed lots of dogs to new owners, I felt sure I'd be able to pick a winner! Everything was perfect.

I had seven hundred Battersea dogs to choose from, which was quite a lot, so I thought long and hard about what kind of dog I wanted. This would help me narrow down my search. I'd decided that I wanted an older dog that had already been trained by someone and who, hopefully, was well-behaved. I walked around the Home looking for my new best friend and wondered which one out of all these hundreds of beautiful and special dogs would eventually win my heart.

As I walked past row upon row of kennels, the puppies and young dogs all jumped up at the bars. 'Pick me, pick me!' they seemed to be saying.

'Sorry, boys and girls,' I said to them. 'I'm looking for someone a little more mature.'

I had never thought about what it must be like for people coming to Battersea to rehome a dog. It was very hard trying to choose just one dog from so many, knowing I couldn't take them all home. I had looked at about half the dogs when I realized my shoelace was undone. I bent down to tie it up and while I was down there I peered into the nearest kennel.

Looking back at me from the same height was a medium-sized mongrel. He was black with a grey face, had pointy ears that flopped over at the ends and the waggiest, bushiest tail I'd ever seen.

'Hello, you!' I said. 'What's your name?' He tilted his head to the left and wagged even harder. 'Sit,' I said. He sat. 'Give paw.' He lifted his right paw and rested it high up on the bars. Then he pushed himself against the door for a stroke. As I stroked his chest through the kennel bars, he rolled over for me to tickle his tummy!

'All right, boy, just let me get in the door!' I said.

As I stood up, I looked at the card clipped to the outside of his kennel.

His name was Gus and he was ten years old. His owner had been sent to prison and that's how Gus had ended up at Battersea.

'You need a home, don't you?' I asked him, unlocking the door. 'Want to come and live with me?' He wagged his tail even harder than before; in fact, his whole bum was wagging now. This was a good sign.

I put Gus on a lead and took him out for a walk. He had been very well-trained and didn't pull at all. He always waited for me to go through doorways first and when I offered him a roast-beef-flavoured Schmacko he even sat without being asked!

I just knew that Gus was the dog for me, so I asked Mr Wadman Taylor to microchip him and then I signed the paperwork and took Gus home with me.

Over the next few days I discovered lots of things about Gus:

- his favourite food was bananas.
- he loved other dogs, especially golden retrievers.
- he was very gentle with cats.
- his favourite game was *fetch*.
- he was terrified of fireworks.
- he didn't like storms.
- he liked to poo in the bushes.
- he *hated* being left alone.

Owning a dog was as brilliant as I had dreamed it would be and Gus and I had so much fun together. Every morning when my alarm went off, Gus would be there to greet me. However sleepy I was feeling, his bright eyes and wagging tail made me want to leap out of bed and go walkies. I think I liked walkies more than he did!

His favourite activity at the park was splashing

around in the pond, but he never liked to go too far out and always made sure he could touch the bottom. The only time he ever went out of his depth was when he got over-excited at the sight of some ducks. He charged in, sending ducks quacking in every direction. He thought this was hilarious until he tried it with a big goose who chased him into the middle of the pond. Gus doggy-paddled for all he was worth and looked relieved to have escaped the fat bird, but his relief turned to panic when he realized he couldn't touch the bottom. Thankfully all dogs can swim so he made it back to shore!

I always took poo bags with me because it is important to be responsible and clear up when your dog does a poo. Gus was a very private sort of a dog and liked to go in the bushes, so sometimes it took a long time to find where he'd been!

Gus loved coming to work with me too, and every morning after breakfast we'd walk across the park to Battersea Dogs Home. Along the way we met lots of other dogs – sometimes the same ones, sometimes new ones. His two favourite four-legged friends were Sally, a golden retriever whom he *loved*, and Dusty, a Border terrier who loved *him*.

His favourite game was playing *fetch* so I always made sure we had a tennis ball with us; if I happened to forget it, any old stick would do.

When we arrived at Battersea, Gus didn't go back into a kennel – from the moment I chose him, his kennel days were over. Instead, he'd settle down in my office for his morning nap.

'It's all right for some,' I said to him. 'You catch up on your sleep while I do all the work!' But I didn't mind. I was rehoming gorgeous dogs to wonderful people so I was happy too.

Every lunch time I raced back to my office, put Gus on a lead and took him to the park to play *fetch* again. Jacky and Rebecca sometimes came too and usually brought three or four dogs from the kennels with them. Gus loved being with other dogs, so they all played happily together until it was time to go back to work.

At the end of the day, Gus and I walked back home, ate our dinner and flopped out in front of the telly until it was time for bed.

He was my best pal. He was always there so I never felt lonely, he made me laugh (sometimes without meaning to!) and we always had the best time together.

But it wasn't all plain sailing . . .

The first time I left Gus alone in my office, he tried to jump out of the window. I wouldn't have minded, but my office was on the first floor! I had only been to the canteen to buy a bacon roll for myself and two sausages for Gus. When I came back towards my office, I looked up to see Gus dangling halfway out of the first-floor window. He had a look of both determination and panic on his face.

I gasped. 'Gus! What are you doing?' I yelled at him, barely able to believe my eyes. 'Stop! Go back!' I shouted, as if he could speak English. I held up both hands (as best as I could without dropping my bacon roll) and gestured for him to reverse.

He was far enough out that I couldn't decide whether to hang on and try and catch him, or race up the stairs and hope I'd be in time to grab him. Catching him would probably have ended up with both of us being injured, so I raced up the stairs three at a time. I flung the door open to find Gus's back legs paddling furiously in midair.

I grabbed them and pulled so that he was now more in than out and gently lifted him down.

'What on earth were you thinking, you silly old fool?' I asked him. He immediately smelled the sausages and instantly forgot all about his great escape. He wolfed down the bangers without them even touching the sides. I, on the other hand, had suddenly lost my appetite, so I gave Gus my bacon roll, which he polished off in no time.

I was in a state of shock and flopped down in my chair. Gus thought a rest was a very good idea too and ambled over to his bed. Within a minute he was snoring his head off as though nothing had happened!

The first time I left Gus alone in my house was just as hair-raising. When I returned home from my evening out, I tried to open my front door, but I couldn't. I pushed as hard as I could, but something was in the way. I soon worked out that Gus had pulled the carpet up, which meant I couldn't get in! He was frantically trying to get to *me*, and I was frantically trying to get to *him*!

I pushed with all my might and the door finally swung open, leaving me in a crumpled heap on the floor. Gus came bounding over, wagging his tail, licking my face and sticking his tongue in my ear!

'Gerroff!' I said, but I couldn't help laughing.

I looked around at the flat. As well as the carpet, he had chewed the remote control, my favourite pair of jeans and the lino on the kitchen floor.

'Hmm,' I said to Gus. 'Either we're going to have to solve this little problem or I'll never be able to go out again!'

The next day I asked the rehabilitation team for some advice. They said that Gus was behaving like this because he'd over-bonded with me and couldn't cope without me. *Right*, I thought, *time for a cunning plan*. If Gus hated it when I went out, I'd trick him into thinking I was still there!

The next time I was due to go out, I fed Gus his dinner just before I was ready to leave. Whilst he was in the kitchen, happily stuffing his face, I took some clothes out of the dirty laundry basket and put them on the bathroom floor. I then grabbed my mobile phone and began replaying on loudspeaker a long conversation I'd recorded into it earlier in the week. I left the phone playing in the bathroom, closed the bathroom door and, while Gus was still eating his food, I set a camcorder to record him. Finally I silently sneaked out of the front door.

I came home a few hours later, a little worried about what I'd find. Had my plan worked? I put my key in the door and slowly pushed it. It opened; the carpet hadn't been pulled up or chewed.

'OK, so far so good,' I said, looking around at the rest of the flat. Nothing had been touched and I found Gus asleep outside the bathroom door.

'Hello, fella,' I said to him. 'What have you been up to then?' He tilted his sleepy head to one side. 'Let's have a look at the video and find out, shall we?' He seemed to like that idea as he came bounding over to me.

I couldn't wait to replay the tape from the camcorder and what I saw made me smile.

I saw myself leaving the flat and I intently watched as Gus finished his food and came looking for me. He saw I wasn't in the kitchen, living room or bedroom. He looked like he was getting a little panicky and was probably even thinking about ripping up the carpet, but instead decided to check the bathroom. This is where the plan came into action. Thanks to my mobile-phone recording, he heard me talking. He tilted his head to one side and then he sniffed at the bottom of the bathroom door. The old clothes I'd left inside the bathroom on the floor smelled strongly of me, so with all these things in place to trick him, he thought I was in there having a bath!

My plan had worked! I did feel sorry for him though. When I came home poor Gus must have thought he was going mad. He had just watched me walk through the front door and he looked from me to the bathroom and then back to me again as if to say, 'Who on earth is in our bath then?'

He shouldn't have mentioned the bath, because a week later he was plonked in it!

It was time for Battersea Dogs Home's Annual Reunion, which meant that Gus had to be looking his very best.

CHAPTER TEN

Party Animals

'Roll up, roll up,' said the man on the microphone. 'Welcome to Battersea Dogs Home's Annual Reunion!'

Each year in September, every dog that has ever set foot inside Battersea Dogs Home is invited to Battersea Park (just around the corner from the Home) for a day of fun and frolics.

'Enter your dog into one of our many competitions,' he continued, pointing at a large, colourful sign listing all the different contests. There was:

- Fancy Dress for Dogs
- Dog that Looks Most Like its Owner
- Dog with the Waggiest Tail
- Dandiest Dog of the Day

I looked around the park and saw hundreds and hundreds of dogs looking happy, healthy and loved, with proud, smiling owners at the other end of their leads. And I was no exception, with the freshly bathed (and now shining) Gus at the end of my lead.

All these dogs were once resident at the world's most famous dogs home, looked after by the kennel maids, veterinary staff and rehabilitation team and then being sent to loving homes by the rehomers. I thought my heart was going to burst at the sight of so many happy, heavenly hounds.

Besides the dogs and their owners, I spied

ice-cream vans, a bouncy castle, a huge dog bath (which Jacky was standing next to with a big apron on), a tent for microchipping and clipping doggy claws (which Mr Wadman Taylor was manning), a stall selling Battersea Dogs Home souvenirs with Rebecca behind the counter and a face-painting stall where doggy faces were the most popular choice.

I also saw a hot dog tent, and seeing as it was lunch time I ambled over to get one.

When I walked into the tent I didn't see sausages or buns, however. There were no onions frying, no mustard or tomato ketchup, either. Instead, it was a cool, air-conditioned tent where people could bring dogs that had got too hot in the summer sunshine!

Inside was a snorting bulldog, a very hairy, hot-looking Old English sheepdog and an overweight cocker spaniel, all of whom seemed to be enjoying the cool air.

Gus and I wandered outside again in search of something to eat, and in a large roped-off area in front of us we found four flaming hoops that police dogs were jumping through. They were all very handsome and totally fearless to be leaping through rings of fire. I decided they must be very good at their police duties.

We found a burger stall and I bought one each for Gus and me. We walked over to the huge bath, which was now occupied by an enormous Irish wolfhound. He was just starting a whopping shake, but he was so big that Jacky's attempt to stop it failed miserably and she was soaked from head to toe!

I turned to walk away so she wouldn't see me giggling and tripped over something small but very solid. My burger went flying, but was quickly hoovered up by Gus. I looked down, and whom should I see but Buster the Jack Russell terrier! He had been waiting patiently at my feet to say hello and I hadn't seen him!

'Buster! Hello, boy,' I said, bending down to give him a cuddle. He crawled into my lap and planted a big wet smacker on my face.

'He remembers you!' said his owners.

'And I certainly remember him!' I said. 'How are you getting on with him?'

'Well,' they replied, 'you have to stay one step ahead of him, but we're good at that, so he's been a little darling.' And looking down at him I could see he was.

'You must be doing something right,' I said. 'I got the photo you sent me of Buster winning the trophy for best-trained dog! Any more competitions coming up?'

'He's in the Dandiest Dog competition later today,' said his owners. 'Come along and watch him.'

'I certainly will,' I said, patting Buster goodbye.

In the middle of everything was another large square roped-off area, about half the size of a football pitch. This was where the judging would take place and where I'd see Buster later on, but right now it was time for the Doggy Fancy Dress.

I couldn't believe what I was seeing:

- a sandy-coloured terrier in a red cape dressed as Superman.
- a poodle wearing a crown, dressed as the Queen.
- a Jack Russell with two long bread buns either side of him dressed as a hot dog (he should have been in the hot dog tent!).
- a Staffy dressed as Harry Potter (complete with glasses and lightning scar).
- and a group of friends who had dressed their eight dogs as Snow White and the Seven Dwarfs!

'Laydees and gentlemen, boyyys and girrrrls,' began the man on the microphone. 'After careful consideration, our judges have chosen a winner,' he said, building the tension. All the owners were adjusting their dogs' costumes and grooming their fur. The crowd fell silent; they couldn't wait to hear the outcome.

'And the winner of the fancy dress is . . .'

Everyone held their breath.

'*Suuupppeerrrrrmannnnn!*'

The sandy-coloured terrier's family cheered with joy and he leaped into their arms, his red cape flowing behind him!

Away from the drama of the ring, lots of other events were happening at the same time, one of which was called 'Temptation Alley'. I wasn't sure what happened here, but there was lots of shouting and excitement and a big queue to take part, so Gus and I went over to see what all the fuss was about.

Mickey was manning this stall and I watched as she held an over-excited Labrador at the starting line whilst its owner walked down to the other end of the long, straight course. When the owner got there she began frantically calling the Labrador over to her. Then it all became clear. He had to run straight to his owner without wandering off anywhere else.

What could be simpler? But all along the floor, between the dog and its owner, I could see all sorts of tasty temptations like sausages, burgers and every dog's favourite: roast-beef-flavoured Schmackos. If the Lab went straight to its owner he won a prize; if he was tempted by any of the food along the way, the owner had to give Battersea Dogs Home a donation. I could see that Battersea was going to make plenty of money from Temptation Alley!

Many dogs that used to be at Battersea were enjoying a day out at the park, but what about the poor dogs that were inside Battersea Dogs Home? They were not forgotten, and although all seven hundred couldn't be brought over, the staff brought some of the ones that were struggling to find a home. These dogs may have needed very experienced owners, or they may simply have needed to live in the country, with wide open spaces to run around in. There were so many people at the reunion, there was bound to be someone just right for every dog.

The dogs were led into the main ring where everyone could see them. Rebecca must have taken a break from her stall because I spied her proudly walking a Jack Russell terrier around the ring. It must be another Buster she'd taken a shine to! Just like Gus, all of these dogs had been bathed and groomed especially for the big day and were looking their very best. The man on the microphone told the crowd all about them, and if anyone was interested in giving any of them a home, they could speak to a rehomer who would find out if they were right for that particular dog.

Just then, out of the corner of my eye, I saw something big, black and hairy charging towards me. *What on earth . . . ?* I turned to face the oncoming inky missile and saw that in its mouth was a hat, flapping in the wind. I immediately knew who it was.

'Roscoe!' I yelled out to him. 'Come on, boy!' At which his ears went flat against his head, his stride lengthened and he sped even faster towards me. He was flying now, almost as fast as a greyhound, and I was a little worried he wouldn't be able to stop in time. I was right. As he reached me, he leaped into my arms, causing me to fall hard onto the ground. Gus wasn't sure what to make of it all!

For a second I must have passed out. I woke up to find two big black paws either side of my head, a cold nose in my left eye and a wet, soggy tongue all over my face. James and Sarah were peering down at me.

'Are you all right?' they asked, with concerned looks upon their faces.

'Oh my goodness, Roscoe!' was all I could say. They helped me up and dusted me down.

'As soon as he saw you, he got loose from the lead and there was no stopping him!' they said. I didn't even mind; being run over by Roscoe was the best part of my day so far.

Just when I thought the day couldn't get any better, I saw Tulip, the mad bus-hopping mongrel. I strode over to her, kneeled down and the two of us had a big hug.

Gus, whose favourite dogs were golden retrievers – remember, Tulip was part golden retriever, which is why I'd originally named her 'Goldie' – suddenly perked up. I think it was love at first sight for both of them and they looked lovingly at each other like an old married couple!

'How is she?' I asked Tulip's owner. 'Any more unsupervised trips into London?'

'No, but I was a little worried coming here today,' she said, laughing. 'We had to get the bus!' Tulip was ancient by now, and although she was looking well I think her days of adventure were well and truly behind her!

An announcement came over the loudspeakers: 'Ladies and gentlemen, boys and girls, it's time for the 'Dog that Looks Most Like its Owner' competition. Please make your way over to the main ring.'

I couldn't possibly miss this!

What greeted me was the funniest thing I'd ever seen. There was:

- a lady with big, frizzy grey hair standing next to her Old English Sheepdog. Both had a pink ribbon in their hair!
- a man with brown hair, a flat nose and a squashed-up face, wearing boxing gloves, standing next to his brown boxer dog.
- a tall lady with a long nose and long blond hair parted in the middle, stroking her Afghan hound.
- a little girl with big curly hair that was so blonde it was almost white. She was wearing a big white woolly jumper and sitting next to her white poodle.

But the winner of 'The Dog that Looks Most Like its Owner' competition was a boy wearing a black-and-white spotty jumper and whose face was painted white with black spots.

He even had black whiskers stuck to his face and looked just like his Dalmatian dog!

Now that the Fancy Dress, the Dog that Looks Most Like its Owner and the Dog With the Waggiest Tail (which was won by a Staffordshire bull terrier that wagged his tail so hard he almost took off into orbit), had taken place it was time for the Dandiest Dog of the Day competition.

This was the biggest prize of all and there were about fifty dogs – all different shapes, sizes and colours – taking part. I saw Tulip, Roscoe and Buster and silently wished them luck. All the while, I was aware of some squealing going on towards the left-hand side of the ring. It sounded like a pig stuck down a hole! I looked over to find out who was making all that noise and was delighted to see my old friend Pepe Le Pew. He was squealing because he'd seen me, but couldn't get to me.

I raced over to him and he leaped up to the same height as me!

'Whoa, boy!' I said. 'Take it easy.' And I bent

down to his level to give him a stroke. He'd been bathed, which I knew he wouldn't have liked much, but he was gleaming from head to toe. His white bits were dazzling and his black bits were shining for all to see.

'Don't you look handsome?' I said, giving him one of his favourite roast-beef treats. 'Now show the judge your very best sit,' I said.

The judge for the Dandiest Dog of the Day had to be a very important person. There could only be one man for the job, so Mr Wadman Taylor strode into the centre of the ring and began casting his expert eye over all of the dogs. It was hard to know which of them I wanted to win; I loved Tulip, Roscoe, Buster and Pepe all so much . . .

After twenty minutes, Mr Wadman Taylor had made his decision.

'And now, the moment you've all been waiting for . . .' the man on the microphone announced. I looked around the park. There were about a thousand people watching the ring now, most of whom had their own dogs with them, all excitedly waiting. The crowd held its breath, waiting for the announcement. There was total silence. Even the dogs were quiet; perhaps they sensed something big was about to happen.

I looked at Roscoe, the hat planted firmly in his mouth, his black coat gleaming in the late summer sun. Tulip was having a little kip, but I saw Pepe giving his very best sit and I watched Buster who, to my surprise, was probably the best-behaved dog in the whole ring! I crossed everything, hoping one of them would win – but there were forty-six other dogs, all looking just as splendid as my four favourites.

Mr Wadman Taylor handed the man on the microphone a piece of paper.

'And now, ladies and gentlemen, boys and girls, and of course all you lovely dogs, it is time to award the biggest prize of all: the trophy for the Dandiest Dog of the Day. Our judge Mr Wadman Taylor has made his decision and the judge's decision is final . . .'

I looked at my four favourites again. 'Please let it be one of them . . .' I said quietly to myself.

The man on the microphone read what was written on the piece of paper, took a deep breath and began marching over towards a splendid-looking springer spaniel standing next to Roscoe. But the closer he got, I realized it was *Roscoe* he was actually heading for.

'The Battersea Dogs Home Annual Reunion Dandiest Dog of the Day is . . .'

No one moved, no one spoke, no one breathed.

'. . . Roscoe!' the man bellowed down his microphone.

'YES!' I shrieked, leaping in the air. The crowd went wild, cheering, and I watched James throw Roscoe's hat up in the air. Roscoe had won my heart all those years ago and now he'd won the crowd's too. Sarah screamed with delight and, sensing the family joy, Roscoe joined in and leaped into James's arms, almost causing him to collapse! Sarah held the cup high and the whole crowd, including me, roared our approval.

Second and third prizes were awarded to Pepe Le Pew and Buster, and Tulip got a special prize for being the oldest dog at the Reunion.

At that moment I was the happiest person in the park – my four favourite dogs had all won a prize. But as I looked down at Gus, I realized that wasn't the only reason I was grinning from ear to ear.

Not only did I have the world's best-ever job, but I also had the world's best-ever dog!

When I left school all those years ago, I was very upset that I couldn't become what I really wanted to be. I'd tried hard in class and did the best I could, but I just wasn't clever enough to be a vet. Luckily it hadn't taken me long to work out that I didn't have to be a vet in order to help the animals I loved so much.

I adored working at Battersea Dogs Home

and I stayed there for a very long time, nearly half my life, in fact.

During that time, almost *a quarter of a million dogs* came through the doors. You could fill Wembley Stadium nearly three times over with that many dogs! And that many Border collies lined up nose to tail would stretch around an Olympic running track 625 times!

Most of those dogs ended up at Battersea because people hadn't thought about the commitment involved in owning a dog. Dogs can live for up to fifteen years and the decision to have one must *never* be taken lightly.

I feel very lucky that I was able to help so many dogs, because to me they represent all that is good about life and the world and humans too.

They are warm, friendly, loving and honest.

They make us laugh, never get tired of playing, and if you're lucky enough to have a dog, you'll never be lonely.

That is why, in my eyes, they are perfect.

NAME: Tulip

BREED: Part mongrel, part Golden Retriever

Golden Retriever characteristics:

* Super-friendly
* Playful
* Eager to please
* Never really grow up!

Tulip's very own special quirks:

* Likes riding on buses
* Will do anything for a sticky bun
* Excellent swimmer
* Loves the postman

NAME: Roscoe

BREED: Part Labrador,
part German
Shepherd

Labrador characteristics:

* Happy dogs
* Friendly with everything and everyone
* Supposed to be energetic but can also be lazy!

German Shepherd characteristics:

* Loyal
* Self-confident
* Strong & athletic

Roscoe's very own special quirks:

* Likes watching TV, especially BBC1
* Only drinks tea from a saucer
* Prefers to sleep under a blanket
* Loves anyone wearing a hat

NAME: Pepe Le Pew

NAME: Quick/Boss

BREED: Border Collie

Border Collie characteristics:

* Super-intelligent
* Super-energetic
* Hard working
* Desperate to please

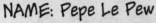

Pepe's very own special quirks:

* Loves curry
* Frightened of the hoover
* Best frisbee catcher in the park

Quick/Boss's very own special quirks:

* Eats horse poo (if allowed to)
* Herds buses (if allowed to)
* Sleeps on the sofa (if allowed to)

NAME: Benjamin

BREED: Lurcher

Lurcher characteristics:

* Very affectionate towards people
* Love to run and chase
* Energetic and agile
* Fun-loving

Benjamin's very own special quirks:

* Loves the Queen
* Will do anything for a chocolate biscuit (and the Queen)
* Adores his family's granny (thinks she's the Queen)
* Favourite football team : Queens Park Rangers

NAME: Buster

BREED: Jack Russell terrier

Jack Russell characteristics:

* Determined
* Always on the go
* Bags of fun
* Big personality despite small size

Buster's very own special quirks:

* Loves digging up flower beds
* Excellent at skateboarding
* Snores in bed
* Hates the postman

NAME: Gus

BREED: Mongrel

Mongrel characteristics:

* Friendly
* Intelligent
* Loveable
* Hardy

Gus's very own special quirks:

* Loves fruit salad
* Howls to the *Eastenders* theme tune
* Is kind to cats
* Terrified of frogs

THE TOTALLY TRUE STORY OF

DEVON

The Naughtiest Dog in the World

Jon has always enjoyed a peaceful life. But when he
agrees to give a home to Devon, an abandoned little
Border collie, things will never be the same again!

From the moment mischievous Devon explodes
out of his cage at the airport, Jon realizes there's
going to be trouble. And over the course of the
next year, he finds out just how much trouble
one little dog can be!

Chasing buses, herding sheep and stealing
meatballs — read all about these and Devon's
other naughty adventures in this wonderful
real-life story.

ISBN: 978 1 849 41110 3

ROSE & IZZY

The Cheekiest Dogs on the Farm

Looking after the dogs, sheep, donkeys, hens, rooster and cat on Bedlam Farm is hard work! But Jon is lucky enough to have Rose, the brave Border collie always at his side.

When Jon hears about Izzy, an abandoned dog kept alone in a field, he can't bear to leave him and agrees to take him in. Life is just about to get even busier!

But Jon soon realizes that cheeky little Izzy is a problem that even Rose can't help him with!

Read all about how Izzy copes with his new life on the farm in this fantastic true story.

ISBN: 978 1 849 41278 0